ANXIETY

IN RELATIONSHIPS

Free Yourself From The Grasp Of Jealousy, Insecurity, And Fear Of Abandonment While Letting Go Of Negative Thinking That May Destroy Your Personal Relation With Your Partner

Elizabeth Davis

Table of Contents

Introduction

nxiety is a common and ongoing experience, as every human being will feel anxious at some point in their lives. However, anxiety can be problematic for some individuals as it interferes with daily functioning. These individuals are typically diagnosed with an anxiety disorder; however, some people have normal anxiety levels but are still impacted by it. This includes those with social phobia.

Social phobia is the third most common mental illness in North America (depression and alcoholism are first and second, respectively). It is estimated to affect between 3–7% of the population (about 15 million). People with social phobia experience three cognitive/somatic, behavioral, and physiological symptoms. Cognitive symptoms of social phobia include heightened self-awareness, rumination, and anticipation of negative evaluation. Somatic symptoms include excessive blushing, heart racing, and sweating.

Behavioral symptoms include avoiding people and social situations. Physiological symptoms include feeling faint, dizzy, or nauseous. Social phobia can be thought of as a spectrum disorder (much like autism), with the most severe cases being diagnosed with a specific phobia (e.g., claustrophobia), while less severe cases fit the diagnostic criteria for social phobia.

The cognitive-behavioral theory is used to explain how anxiety disorders develop. This theory assumes that thoughts, feelings, and behaviors are interconnected and affect each other reciprocally.

This theory's cognitive component is as follows:

- An individual has a thought, feeling, or behavior (negative appraisal).

- The person is aware of the negative thoughts/feeling.

- Negative self-awareness.

- Behavioral avoidance.

For example, a man who becomes anxious when speaking in public will feel self-conscious about his anxiety symptoms. This leads him to avoid public speaking situations, reinforcing his belief that he cannot handle these situations effectively.

Cognitive-behavioral theory can also be used to explain how social phobia develops. The cognitive component of social phobia is the assumption that everyone must like a person; this thought may be unrealistic, but it reinforces feelings of self-consciousness and worthlessness. This leads to avoidant behaviors, reinforcing the idea that nothing can be changed. The cognitive-behavioral theory has also been used to explain many types of anxiety disorders, including panic disorder and generalized anxiety disorder.

Social phobia developed due to maladaptive learning and association with one's environment (internalizing and externalizing factors). According to Beck's cognitive model, internalizing factors, such as negative self-evaluation, are associated with social phobia. It could stem from early life experiences (e.g., parents or significant others) and beliefs acquired during childhood. Beck (1976) developed the cognitive model to assess the primary factors related to depression, anxiety disorders, and alcoholism. The model argues that negative cognitions, which are generally acquired in childhood, are the underlying causes of anxious thoughts, which lead to physiological arousal.

In terms of externalizing factors leading to social phobia, a social phobia may respond to an external stimulus or situation. This theory is known as the "behavioral view." This viewpoint argues a child with social phobia will tend to avoid potentially traumatic situations; these situations may include family members or peers who are critical, cold, or indifferent. The child's feelings about these interactions are considered (i.e., the child believes he is a bad person, uncaring or stupid), reinforcing avoidance of subsequent situations. Also, a social phobia may stem from family dynamics (i.e., an overly critical mother). Many factors may be associated with social phobia, including emotional abuse and neglect as a child or adolescent and a family history of alcoholism or depression.

According to the behavioral theory of social phobia, avoidance results in reinforcement and thus increases the likelihood that an individual will behave in this manner again. Fear of negative evaluation is known as "social anxiety," which causes people to avoid people or social situations. The fear of negative evaluation created by social anxiety leads to more avoidance and more reinforcement of the behavior (i.e., feeling uncomfortable, fleeing, or withdrawing from the situation).

Many researchers have questioned the behavioral theory of social phobia because it cannot account for several symptoms experienced in social phobias, such as physiological distress (anxiety is suggested to be caused by avoidance and reinforces it), which are not underlined conscious control. The "behavioral" view also does not consider the role of certain cognition factors that may lead to an initial anxiety response, such as misinterpretation or unrealistic expectation.

CHAPTER 1:

Anxiety in general

The American Psychological Association (APA) specifies anxiousness as "a feeling characterized by sensations of stress, stressed ideas and physical modifications like enhanced blood pressure." Understanding the difference between normal sensations of anxiety and an anxiety disorder calling for clinical attention can help an individual identify and treat the problem. Everybody feels distressed now and then. It's a common emotion. For example, you may contact worried when faced with trouble at the office, before taking a test, or before making a vital choice. Stress and anxiety conditions are different, though. They are a group of mental diseases, and the distress they trigger can maintain you from carrying on with your life regularly. For individuals who have one, worry and anxiety are constant and frustrating and can be disabling. However, with therapy, many individuals can take care of those sensations and get back to a satisfying life. When an individual encounters possibly harmful or distressing triggers, feelings of stress and anxiety are not just typical, but necessary for survival.

Since the earliest days of humankind, the predators' method and incoming threat trigger alarms in the body and enable incredibly elusive activity. These alarm systems become noticeable in the form of an elevated heartbeat, sweating, and boosted sensitivity to environments. The risk causes a rush of adrenalin, a hormone and chemical messenger in the mind, which triggers these anxious responses in a procedure called the "fight-or-flight" reaction. This prepares people to physically confront or leave any potential hazards to safety and security. For many individuals, ranging from bigger pets and an impending threat is a much less important issue than it would have been for very early human beings. Stress and anxieties currently revolve around the job, cash, domesticity, wellness, and other important issues that demand a person's focus without always calling for the "fight-or-flight" response. Before a vital life occasion or throughout a difficult situation, the anxious sensation is an all-natural echo of the initial 'fight-or-flight' reaction. It can still be essential to survival—anxiety about being struck by a car when crossing the street, for example, means that an individual will naturally look at both methods to avoid the threat. Stress and anxiety are your body's all-natural actions to stress and anxiety. It's a sensation of concern or worry concerning what will be ahead. On the first day of the institution, going to a job interview or providing a speech might trigger many people to feel scared and worried. Yet if your feelings of stress and anxiety are severe, last longer than six months, and get in the way of your life, you might have an anxiety condition.

Anxiety through the centuries

If we had lived in the 14th or 15th century, we would certainly most likely have used the terms stress and anxiety. However, with 1 or 2 significant exceptions, it would undoubtedly have had little to do with our mental state, other than probably with effects. Anxiety had to do with adversity, challenge, or some form of ailment even more. It was not until the 18th and 19th centuries that a shift in meaning began to occur. As many people understand, the 18th and 19th centuries are connected with a duration of intense clinical and commercial development. As scientific research developed, language adapted to accommodate and articulate these adjustments. The physical sciences, most significantly engineering, started to use terms like tension, strain, resilience, stress, and elasticity to define materials' results. Almost everyone will undoubtedly recognize these as expressions typically used within medication and psychology. Still, others, like snapping or breaking factor, tend not to be used within the occupations these days. However, they maintain a position in daily language relating to feelings or behavior.

CHAPTER 2:

Different types of anxiety disorder

Generalized anxiety disorder

Feeling anxious and stressed from time to time is common, particularly if your life is challenging. However, a symptom of generalized anxiety disorder may be excessive, persistent anxiety and concern that are difficult to manage and interfere with daily tasks. As an infant or an adult, it is likely to experience a generalized anxiety disorder. There are signs of generalized anxiety disorder that are identical to panic disorder, obsessive-compulsive disorder, and other anxiety forms, yet these are also distinct disorders. Living with a generalized anxiety disorder may be a struggle in the long run. It happens associated with other mood or anxiety problems in many situations.

Signs and symptoms

A sign of generalized anxiety disorder may differ. They can contain:

- Persistent fear or anxiety over various areas that are out of comparison to the result of the accidents.

- Difficulty in concentration, or the sense that the mind goes blank.

- Perceiving circumstances and incidents as harmful, even though they are not.

- Overthinking solutions and plans for all potential worst-case results.

- Trouble managing confusion.

- Failure to put worry aside or let go.

- Fear and indecisiveness of making the incorrect option.

- Feeling nervous, unwilling to sleep, and feeling up or on the edge of the key.

Physical symptoms and signs can include:

- Tiredness.

- Muscle Ache Or Muscle Tension.

- Irritability.

- Sleep Problems.

- Feeling Twitchy Or Trembling.

- Sweating.

- Nervousness Or Getting Startled Quickly.

- Diarrhea, Nausea, Or Condition With Irritable Bowel.

There might be occasions when you are not overwhelmed by your fears, but you always feel nervous even when there is no apparent cause. For instance, you may have a deep fear for your welfare or that of your family members, or you could have a general feeling that something terrible will happen. Physical signs, anxiety, or concern trigger your considerable distress in social, job, or other aspects of your life. Worries can change from one issue to another, and over time and maturity, they can change.

Symptoms in teenagers and children

Children and teens may have joint issues with those of adults but may also have excessive concerns about:

- School results or sports activities.

- Being on time or punctual.

- Security of family members.

- Nuclear war, other catastrophic events, or earthquakes.

A child or teenager with extreme anxiety can:

- Sound overly eager to blend in.

- Redoing activities because the first time they are not fine.

- Wants to be a perfectionist.

- Excessive time spent on homework.

- Lack of confidence.

- Strive for consent.

- Needs a lot of reassurance regarding progress.

- Avoid attending college or preventing social conditions.

- Have regular stomachaches or other medical problems.

Post-traumatic anxiety or stress disorder

(PTSD) Post-traumatic stress disorder is a mental health problem caused by either suffering or watching a terrifying occurrence. Symptoms, and some uncontrollable feelings regarding the incident, can involve hallucinations, extreme distress, and nightmares. Many people who go through stressful experiences can have temporary trouble adapting and managing, but they typically get stronger over time and proper self-care. You could have PTSD if the effects worsen, persist for months or years, and interact with day-to-day functioning.

Signs and symptoms

Post-traumatic stress disorder symptoms can begin within one month after a traumatic experience, but symptoms may not occur until years after the incident, often. In work or social conditions and marriages, these signs trigger critical difficulties. They can even mess with your willingness to perform your everyday activities normally. Symptoms of PTSD are commonly classified into four types: recurring memories, pessimistic shifts of attitude and thought, avoidance, and shifts of emotional and physical pain. Symptoms may differ with time or vary from individual to individual.

Intruding memories

Intruding or intrusive memory signs can include:

- Unwanted recurrent unpleasant memories of the traumatic incident.

- Upsetting visions or nightmares about a painful experience.

- Reliving the painful experience as if it were occurring (flashbacks) again.

- Extreme psychiatric illness or bodily responses to something that triggers you of a painful experience.

Adverse changes in mood and thinking

Symptoms of harmful changes in perception and attitude may involve:

- Difficulty having positive thoughts.

- Negative feelings regarding yourself, the world, or other people.

- Problems in a recall, like not recalling major details of the stressful experience.

- Hopelessness regarding the future.

- Feeling separated from friends and relatives.

- Difficulty in keeping strong relations.

- Lack of motivation you once enjoyed in things.

- Feeling numb emotionally.

Avoidance

Avoidance signs can include:

- Avoiding events, sites, or persons that remind you of a traumatic experience.

- Trying not to remember or speak about the painful experience.

Changes in emotional and physical reactions

Symptoms of improvements (also termed as arousal symptoms) in emotional and physical pain can include:

- Easily startled or terrified.

- Concentrating difficulty.

- Self-destructive actions, such as over-drinking or moving too rapidly.

- It is always being on guard for danger.

- Sleeping trouble.

- Irritability, aggressive behavior, or angry outbursts.

- Overwhelming shame or guilt.

Symptoms and signs can also contain the following for children six years old and younger:

- Scary visions that may or may not contain components of a stressful experience.

- Re-enacting, by play, the traumatic incident or facets of the traumatic experience.

The intensity of signs and symptoms

Symptoms of PTSD can differ in severity over time. When you're depressed or even when you run across memories about what you passed through, you might experience more PTSD signs.

For instance, you can hear a car backfire and then relive fighting experiences or you might see an article about a sexual attack on the television and feel overwhelmed by your own attack experiences.

Obsessive-compulsive disorder

The obsessive-compulsive disorder known as OCD has a history of unwanted feelings and worries (obsessions) that contribute to repeated (compulsive) activities. Such compulsions and obsessions interfere with day-to-day tasks and trigger significant anxiety. You can attempt to disregard your habits or avoid them, but that just raises your depression and anxiety. Ultimately, you feel compelled to commit compulsive actions to relieve the discomfort. They keep on coming back despite attempts to ignore or get rid of problematic feelings or impulses. This vicious circle of OCD contributes to more ritualistic actions. OCD also circles such subjects as the irrational apprehension of germ exposure. To relieve your fears of infection, you can wash your hands compulsively until they are sore and chapped. You may be embarrassed and ashamed about the disorder if you have OCD, but therapy may be successful.

Signs and symptoms

The obsessive-compulsive disorder typically encompasses compulsions as well as obsessions. But you can also only have symptoms of obsession or just symptoms of compulsion. You may or may not know that your compulsions and obsession are irrational or excessive. Still, they consume a lot of time and disrupt the operation of your everyday life and social, education, or job.

Obsession symptoms

Unwanted, repeated, and intense feelings, desires, or images that are distracting and causing panic or anxiety are OCD obsessions. By doing a compulsive activity or ritual, you may attempt to avoid them or to get rid of them. These obsessions usually intrude when you're attempting to conceive about or do other stuff.

Obsessions provide themes with them sometimes, such as:

- Fear of dirt or contamination.

- Unwanted feelings, like violence, or topics of sex or faith.

- Need for things to be orderly and symmetrical.

- Doubtful and having trouble tolerating misunderstanding.

- Violent or horrible feelings of losing power and hurting oneself or anyone.

Examples of the symptoms and signs of obsession include:

- Fear of being infected by handling items touched by others.

- Extreme tension when objects are not orderly or in any way facing.

- Doubts that you have the door closed or the stove switched off.

- Pictures of driving a vehicle through a mass of individuals.

- Uncomfortable sexual videos.

- Thoughts on yelling obscenities or inappropriately behaving in public.

- Avoidance of conditions that may trigger obsessions, like trembling hands.

Compulsion symptoms

Repetitive habits that you are compelled to continue are OCD compulsions.

These repeated habits or behavioral actions are supposed to relieve discomfort or avoid something unpleasant from occurring, linked to your obsessions. However, participating in the compulsions provides little gratification and can only provide brief relief from anxiety.

When you experience obsessive feelings, you might think up guidelines or habits to obey to help regulate your anxiety. These compulsions are unhealthy and are sometimes not connected to the issue they are supposed to address.

Compulsions, as with obsessions, usually include themes, such as:

- Cleaning and washing.

- Following a strict schedule.

- Counting.

- Checking.

- Orderliness.

- Demanding security.

Examples of signs and effects of compulsion include:

- Washing your hands until you have raw skin.

- Repeating a word, prayer, or phrase quietly.

- Repeatedly testing the stove to ensure that it is off.

- Repeatedly locking doors to ensure they're closed.

- Counting in particular patterns.

- Arrange the canned food in the same way to face the same.

Variety in severity

In the adolescent or young adult years, OCD typically starts, although it may begin in childhood. Symptoms usually start progressively and across life appear to differ in intensity. Over time, the kinds of compulsions and obsessions that you encounter will also shift. When you undergo more significant discomfort, symptoms usually worsen. OCD may have mild to moderate effects, typically called a lifelong condition, or it may be so extreme and time-intensive that it has become disabling.

Social anxiety

In specific social settings, it's natural to feel anxious. For instance, the sensation of butterflies in the stomach may be triggered by going on a date or making a presentation. However, daily encounters induce substantial distress, fear, self-consciousness, and embarrassment in social anxiety disorder, often called social phobia, since your paranoia about being scrutinized or evaluated by others. Anxiety and fear in social anxiety disorder contribute to avoidance that may ruin your life. Your everyday life, career, education, or other hobbies may be influenced by extreme stress. A persistent mental health problem is a generalized anxiety disorder, but developing coping strategies through psychotherapy and getting medications will help you build confidence and strengthen the capacity to communicate with others.

Signs and symptoms

Feelings of discomfort or shyness in some environments, particularly in children, are not usually symptoms of social anxiety disorder. Trust levels in social settings differ based on individual qualities and life experiences. Naturally, certain persons are quiet while others are more outgoing.

In comparison to ordinary nervousness, social anxiety disorder involves anxiety, paranoia, and isolation that interfere with regular life, work, education, or other hobbies.

Physical signs and symptoms

A social anxiety disorder may also be followed by physical signs and symptoms and can include:

- Blushing.

- Tremble.

- Heart Beating Fast.

- Transpiration.

- Difficulties Holding Your Breath.

- Tension In The Muscles.

- Lightheadedness Or Dizziness.

- Stomach Upset Or Nausea.

- Feeling Your Mind's Gone Blank.

Behavioral And Emotional Symptoms

Persistent symptoms or signs of social anxiety disorder may include:

- Fear in circumstances where you may be criticized.

- Worrying about yourself being ashamed or insulted.

- Expecting the worst potential outcomes during a social situation from an adverse event.

- Fear of someone thinking that you appear anxious.

- To stop doing stuff or communicating with persons out of fear of humiliation.

- In preparation for a feared event or occurrence, possessing anxiety.

- Spending time assessing your results and finding weaknesses in your relationships after a social scenario.

Performance-type social anxiety disorder is when extreme fear and anxiety are felt only during public speaking or acting, but not in any kind of social circumstances.

CHAPTER 3:

How anxiety could reflect on us and our relationships

Anxiety can influence an individual's life in many ways, including affecting the relationship with family and friends, their love life, and even work. Some people don't understand how anxiety functions. Educating people about mental conditions is critical. Also, though anxiety can't be seen, it's real. Many people don't even think there are anxiety disorders and mental disorders. This doesn't necessarily go away just by accepting it, but it does help to get diagnosed and treated. For some instances, if left untreated, it can get even worse.

There are various kinds of anxiety disorders, but they all include experiencing the same sort of intense fear that can lead to function and behavior issues. Social anxiety significantly affects some people, which may affect how relationships are shaped and established. When anyone has anxiety in a relationship, it may influence the relationship.

Relationship anxiety can lead to overthinking, doubting, questioning your partner's feelings, arguing, and stressing the connection.

Being empathetic is crucial in handling people with anxiety disorders. Understanding that their experience with anxiety is unique to them, providing a listening ear, but most importantly, not pressing people or trying to force solutions on people. One simple thing that someone's partner can do is be considerate and patient with their significant others. Learning more about the disease will strengthen the bond between the two individuals. One should persuade their partner to seek out counseling.

Adverse effects of anxiety on love life

Nonetheless, anxiety should not come in the way of a relationship or place a strain on it to the point that it becomes difficult to enjoy. You will love each other more deeply and communicate differently through knowing anxiety and how it affects people in a relationship.

Educating yourself and the people around you can also alleviate tremendous tension. Most people have a couple of nervous thoughts. They are a normal part of being in a relationship, especially a new relationship.

Nevertheless, people with anxiety disorders appear to have such nervous thoughts more frequently and more deeply. Their ideas take over and go straight to the worst-case scenario. The nervous thoughts cause physiological signs, including shortness of breath, insomnia, and anxiety attack. Someone with anxiety can respond as if the stress was a physical assault. Anxious thoughts often encourage you to behave in ways that stress you and strengthen the relationship. Individuals with anxiety, for example, regularly test the loyalty of their partner by using vulnerable methods. For example, your partner is full of guilt that they are the first to start contact. They begin to worry that you don't like them as much as they like you because you don't send out the first signal as often as they do. The fear intensifies, and they start to feel that if they didn't reach out first, you would never speak with them.

Unfortunately, people experience several anxiety-related behaviors in relationships. Being frustrated, irritated, overwhelmed, and having difficulty concentrating, coming off as overly negative thoughts, and being perfect all the times become part of your life.

Sadly, anxiety will affect your love life for those of us who are hoping to find love. It's terrible because everything seems so perfect, and you want everything to continue to be accurate, but you know that it's only a matter of time before things start to go wrong. This is how it feels like to be in a stable relationship with those of us with anxiety.

It's almost more comforting when things begin to go wrong because your mind has spent so much time preparing for a disaster that it's a relief to know you're not crazy. Your relationship's downfall has always been waiting around the corner.

Your anxiety begins impacting your relationship for the worse, and it's like you can't do anything to stop it. When your relationship is in trouble, the feeling you get is a more vivid kind of anxiety that explodes into your mind and feels much more severe.

Still, the kind you get when everything seems to be just fine is a slow-burning fear that sits in the back of your mind and creates a very subtle type of havoc in your psyche.

Anxiety may trigger periods of panic, anxiety or overwhelming feelings, and a general sense of unease and stress. It can take over your thoughts and make many areas of your life bleed. If you feel a burden on your relationship, anxiety may have a part to play. Is your anxiety or your partner's anxiety putting your relationship in danger? Here's how and why anxiety can ruin your relationship with your partner:

- Anxiety induces fear or concern that can make you less conscious of your real needs. If you're concerned about what could happen, it's hard to pay attention to what's going on.

- Anxiety shatters your inner voice. Anyone who appears to be anxious may find it difficult to communicate their true feelings. It might also be hard to maintain appropriate boundaries when asking for the attention or space needed. Since experiencing anxiety is uncomfortable, you may subconsciously attempt to postpone their experience. On the other hand, anxiety may lead you to feel that something needs to be spoken about immediately when a brief break can be beneficial. If you're not voicing what you think or need, anxiety becomes greater. Plus, if you hold them in, your emotions can inevitably spiral off balance. You could get frustrated and defensive.

- Anxiety may make you behave selfishly. Since anxiety is an overactive reaction to fear, often someone who experiences it may concentrate too much on their worries or problems. Your concerns and fears can bring undue pressure to bear on your relationship. You may feel you need to protect yourself in your relationship, but it will prevent you from being caring and open to your partner. If your partner has anxiety, you can also build up anger and respond selfishly. The behaviors we have and the experiences are infectious. It is especially challenging to keep the stress levels under control when the partner feels nervous, frustrated, or defensive.

- Unhealthy anxiety levels keep you on the emotional edge all the time. Anxiety causes you to dismiss non-hazardous things and avoid things that might benefit you. It can also stop you from taking the right action to change something that hurt you in your life because it makes you feel hopeless or stuck.

- The feeling of happiness requires a sense of protection or independence. Anxiety makes us feel either terrified or impaired. A brain and body conditioned to stress will also have a much harder time enjoying intimacy and sex. Negative thoughts and fears impact a person's ability to be present within a relationship and potentially suck the joy out of a moment.

Adverse effects of anxiety on family and friends

There are ways anxiety can affect one's family life. Specifically, the symptoms one can encounter during an anxiety disorder can involve symptoms such as irritability, stress, lack of healthy sleep, and focus issues—this may affect one's relationships with family members or one's ability to do one's work effectively. It hinders your communication with others.

Anxiety disorders are often co-occurring with other severe psychiatric disorders, particularly familiar, depression, and drug abuse. When you have an anxiety disorder, you are at a considerably higher risk of developing one of the two other conditions that significantly affect relationships and work. Anxiety can place a lot of pressure on relationships, becoming very isolating. Friends and family may also feel depressed or anxious, and they don't want to see you hurting, but they don't always know how to help.

Depending on the symptoms you encounter, anxiety can affect relationships in various ways. To others, it can cause them to rely excessively on their loved ones; some may isolate themselves to fear of being a burden. Here's how anxiety can ruin your relationship with your family and friends:

- Anxiety may often cause you to become excessively dependent. Their anxiety may make them worried about being alone or facing other circumstances by themselves. Anxiety can also create a person to doubt their decisions, which can lead to over-dependence as well. People with anxiety may have a strong need to be close to their friends or spouse and may seek constant support. This can cause social interactions to overthink, causing them to worry about someone not reacting quickly via social media. To prevent negative feelings, some people have the anxiety to avoid relationships (like being upset or irritated with a loved one). It can be challenging to open up to those you are close to and be vulnerable to. Because of that, though you are striving for closeness, others may view you as a cold, stand-off, which makes it extremely difficult, and often impossible, to sustain and establish new ties.

- People with anxiety sometimes feel anxious or irritated, and people around them may feel stressed. When someone has anxiety, others sometimes don't know how to react to it. This stress can cause connection problems and communication problems in relationships.

CHAPTER 4:

Anxiety in relationships

When you experience anxiety, you experience an overactive response to fear; it causes you to focus on yourself and your problems. Your fears and worries can exude unneeded pressure on your relationship when this happens. You feel that your anxiety is necessary to protect yourself and your best interests in the connection when your anxiety is keeping you from being vulnerable and compassionate with your partner. If your partner shows signs of anxiety, you might react selfishly because you have built up resentments and fears.

Entering into a romantic relationship can often feel like you are playing some dangerous game with yourself; you risk being disappointed or even emotionally hurt when seeking companionship from other people. To begin and maintain a meaningful relationship will require you to display a certain amount of vulnerability. You may experience certain anxiety by merely pursuing a relationship because of its unknown and uncertain outcomes. Untreated anxiety disorders can have a profound negative effect on romance. You may always worry about how other people judge you, so you might avoid dating or getting into a relationship to not feel embarrassed or disappointed. If you struggle with fears of abandonment, then you might worry that every future partner will leave you, eventually. You don't need to have an actual anxiety disorder to allow anxiety to ruin your love life. Any common daily fear can become worrying about communicating with a partner, fear of going out on dates, or any generalized worry about the relationship process.

If there is any doubt in your mind that your romantic relationship might be crumbling because of the effects of anxiety, then consider the following questions:

- Do you continuously have fears and worries that your partner is unfaithful to you when the two of you are not together?

- Does the absence of your partner fill you with feelings of dread and anxiety?

- Do your inner fears of conflict and its possible outcome cause you to avoid having severe or intimate conversations with your partner?

- Does intimacy, including sexual intimacy, cause you to experience feelings of dread?

- Do you assume your partner is unfaithful even when you have no evidence that they see someone else?

- Does your partner always need to reassure you and calm your fears and your anxious thoughts?

- Do you fear being left alone and lonely?

Relationship anxiety is widespread, and some of it is perfectly normal, even healthy for the relationship. There is usually some anxiety level at the beginning of a relationship since this is all new territory. You are sailing in uncharted waters. No two relationships are exactly alike, and what worked in the last one might not work in this one. Even relationships of some duration can be hampered by relationship anxiety. The anxiety you feel may not even be related to the relationship itself. Still, it will lead to behaviors that will create your partner's issues and your relationship and problems. These anxieties can lead to physical complaints, emotional exhaustion, a lack of motivation, and complete emotional distress.

Relationship anxiety can make itself known in many different ways. Especially in the early days of the relationship, there will be some insecurity about the relationship's progress. These anxieties usually pass quickly when you see that the other person is truly committed to making this relationship work. But there are also definite signs that you are experiencing relationship anxiety:

You might wonder if you even matter to your partner

One of the most normal manifestations of anxiety in a relationship is wondering about your importance. It brings up those underlying feelings of wondering if your partner will be there for you if they have your best interests in their thoughts. It shows a basic need for the partners to feel secure in their partnership, connect with the other person on a deep level, and feel as though they belong to something special. You may worry that your partner is only there for what you do for them. You might feel like they can't be trusted with severe matters or that they wouldn't even miss you if you were gone.

You may begin to wonder if this relationship is really 'the one'

If you feel anxious about your relationship, you might continuously question your attachment to the other person. You may wonder if this is the partner for you or your relationship. Even if the relationship is going well, you will question every aspect. You will wonder if this relationship is making you happy or if you think it is making you happy. You may focus on the little differences that point to your incompatibility as a couple.

You might spend your time wondering when they will break up with you

We always hope that all the relationships we enter into will be happy, loving affairs. When the time is right, and the people are right, the two partners will feel happy, secure, and loved. You want to hold tightly to these feelings and hope they last forever. In a good relationship, these feelings can last forever. Nevertheless, when anxiety creeps into a relationship, these good feelings will soon be replaced by persistent doubts and fears. You might worry that your partner is planning to leave you. Then you will adjust your behavior to ensure that you will hold their continued affections. You will worry that they may become angry with you for some imagined event, even if they don't seem to be angry about anything. You will keep quiet when your partner does things that bother you instead of speaking up when you need something. And you will avoid discussing any issue that might cause a rift in the relationship.

CHAPTER 5:

Recognize relationship anxiety and how it starts

"Checking out" out of a relationship

One of the most common yet ugly side effects of relationship anxiety is the sense of being absent from your partner even when they are right next to you. Anxiety can make you live in the same house with your partner and still feel absent or lonely. You will not be fully present in your life. Honestly, that feeling sucks, and it will hurt your relationship. First and foremost, anxiety will deprive you of the feeling of being truly connected to your partner. Consequently, you two will have arguments now and then because of the feelings of neglect and disconnect. However, this problem can be fixed. If you know that you have anxiety problems, you can make conscious efforts towards remaining present when spending time with your partner. You can also seek assistance from a therapist or a loved one who will show you different ways of feeling more grounded and dealing with anxiety.

Having trust issues

Anxiety makes things seem out of control in most cases. It can make your relationship appear out of control. As such, you will hardly ever feel secure with your partner. An anxious person tends to be more jealous and insecure in relationships than other people. They will demand to know where the partner is, who they are texting, the calls, social media platforms, et cetera. Such a person will text or call frequently and ask for the partner's exact location and who they are with. They will invade into private space.

Even though the trust issues stem from seemingly valid reasons, they will gradually destroy your relationship. This habit will make your partner second guess things always. That is a good reason you should look for ways to deal with anxiety without affecting your relationship.

Coming off as controlling

People who have anxiety issues will try to control the relationship. This will hurt the relationship. A person who tries to maintain a relationship comes off as manipulative. That might not be your intention—to control your partner—but it will still be difficult for the partner to deal with it for long.

Overthinking

Relationship anxiety will make you overthink things and eventually end the relationship if a solution is not found. If you tend to overthink everything, it is a clear indicator of anxiety, and it will affect your relationship. You need to be concerned about the impact of overthinking in a relationship. The solution to this challenge is basically to stop over editing your life. This might be difficult at first, but with the right guidance and support, you will be able to find a solution to your problem.

Taking things personally

Anxiety in a relationship can make you over rationalize everything and feel that everything that is said or done is directed towards you. Anxiety will make a person jump to conclusions too quickly, and the problem is most of these deductions are negative. The inner critical voice has a way of making everything look gloomy. It makes one assume the worst, even in the best situations.

For instance, if a person suffering from relationship anxiety feels that their partner is distant, they might take it as a sign of loss of interest. So, instead of having a conversation and finding out why the partner is distant, they will conclude that the relationship has become boring. There are various reasons why a person can be distant in a relationship, for instance, stress, depression, physical illness, etc. Still, relationship anxiety will make you think you are the cause. Always try to look for other possible explanations before judging yourself to solve this problem. Ask questions before picking fights or jumping to conclusions. It is okay to pay attention to the relationship issues, but do not let every other issue make you lose your senses.

Staying stuck in the same position

Change is inevitable, and relationships need to grow. To remain healthy, a relationship has to be dynamic. However, a person who experiences relationship anxiety can have a tough time accepting this fact. People with anxiety problems tend to hold back taking risks, try new things, and even get carried away. They like to deal with what they already know and are comfortable with. A spark to ignite the front is vital between two people. If you have relationship anxiety and are afraid of trying new things, make a point of letting things flow. Find new experiences, and let go of the idea of being perfect. Anxiety is only killing your happiness.

Expecting another person to fix problems

Anxiety makes a person want to avoid being held accountable. You do not want to admit a mistake because your partner might find it a good enough reason to leave you. Failing to acknowledge your role in a situation results in a lack of a solution. No one will fix your mistakes apart from you. No one will implement your ideas in your relationship. No one will improve your anxiety problems for you. Not even your partner can resolve your issue unless you commit to sorting it out.

Your partner may know about your challenge with anxiety and may offer support whenever possible, but they will not fix you, and the sooner you realize that, the better it is for you. Putting pressure on them to help you out will only crush the relationship. It is wrong to expect that your partner will always be there to reassure you; they are not responsible for your anxiety. Your partner can't cure your anxiety. That task is yours, and you have to find help. You will be surprised by the kind of relief that relaxing hobbies, such as meditation and yoga can offer.

Passive-aggressive responses

Anxiety leads to irritability feelings, and consequently, you might find yourself responding to a partner passive-aggressively or lashing out at them unnecessarily. Relationship anxiety makes it hard for people to have a conversation—they usually head downhill. This issue can be solved positively by going through therapy, identifying, and resolving the underlying problem.

Unhealthy degrees of venting

As mentioned earlier, anxiety makes things seem out of control. If you are not coping with anxiety appropriately/healthy, do not be surprised if you keep repeating the mistake of complaining or venting to your partner. It is okay to let some of that steam off, but it is wrong to bombard your partner with all sorts of issues. When anxious, people tend to feel overwhelmed, so much so that all they want is to be heard immediately, here and now. However, what is shared under the influence of anxiety are just chaotic speeches. In the same sentence, a person suffering from anxiety will talk about stress at work and the leaking kitchen sink at home. It will be a desperate monologue with the hope of being heard. However, this might break the relationship because the partner will feel burdened and, in turn, tune us out. There are many ways of letting off steam and venting without forcing your partner to face the stress of your life. Take up some physical exercise or soothing practices such as yoga. Spare your relationship.

Doubt

Anxiety will make you always doubt the validity of your relationship and the reliability of your partner. If you find yourself constantly questioning your relationship and its health, take stock of your feelings. What is causing this doubt? Are you feeling anxious, or is there a valid reason?

Anxiety leads to negative self-talk for some people, which makes them not trust people and even themselves. The resulting doubt can make a partner feel frustrated and eventually give up and quit the relationship. Therefore, one needs to find ways of dealing with this insecurity and finally find peace.

Getting unnecessarily angry

Anxiety leads to emotional instability, and consequently, one finds themselves getting more irritable. This irritability snowballs into anger fast if one is not careful. Anger can arise when we feel trapped, panicked, unheard, or unsure, which is very common for people fighting anxiety and panic attacks. Such people could be talking about something important or trying to solve a problem; they get a feeling of anxiety or panic that makes the brain flip and the primary self kick in.

They may lose control over themselves and their verbal skills, thus ending the conversation. This habit sabotages the relationship over time. There are many healthier ways of dealing with anger and related emotions or preventing them from arising. Talking with an understanding loved one can be the first step in dealing with your challenges and visiting a therapist.

CHAPTER 6:

Common behaviors (conscious and unconscious)

Irrational behaviors caused by generalized anxiety disorder (gad)

Among all the anxiety disorders on the list, this is the most common of the lot. Intense and persistent worry is a common symptom associated with GAD. This includes concerns about your relationships in life, regardless of what type of connections you are. Those diagnosed with GAD can persistently worry about several events in their lives, big or small. It could range from work, school, friendships, family life at home, and, yes, romantic relationships. They worry if they'll arrive at work on time when they're stuck in traffic. They worry about paying the bills this month when unexpected expenses have come up. They worry about their health or the health of their loved ones. They worry about how their kids are doing at school. They worry if they'll get the promotion they interviewed for at work. Little bits of worry here and there are typical on an average day. You will find other common behaviors with GAD: fatigue, restlessness, difficulty concentrating on the tasks they are supposed to do. It can be challenging to focus on a conversation, too. For example, your partner (or anyone for that matter) might be talking to you about something, but you find your mind drifting toward your worries again in the middle of the conversation. Those who struggle with GAD will find it challenging to explain their fears to others. Those with more specific anxiety disorders can still demonstrate their concerns using particular examples, but GAD struggles in that department because the fears are general. It's hard to explain why you might worry about everything. Someone who works with GAD is more worried about circumstances and the possibility of more bad things than others. The way they react to the worries they feel would be what others call "blowing things out of proportion."

To others, their behavior might seem unreasonable. After all, why would someone worry about everything when there is no real cause for alarm? But for the GAD sufferer, those fears are genuine. They become increasingly difficult to reason with because their worries have overpowered all sense of logic and reason. It starts with concerns about a specific situation, but slowly that worry extends and grows more significant as they start making connections to other related or similar problems. For example, suppose your partner took too long to reply to your text yesterday because they were caught up in a meeting, and they took too long to respond to your text again today. In that case, GAD might cause you to form irrational connections, linking one situation to the next and creating a disastrous catastrophe in your mind. These connections might not seem relevant or make sense to most people, but it's a genuine cause for alarm to those with GAD.

Irrational behaviors caused by social anxiety disorder (sad)

Those who struggle with SAD can get to a point where they feel physically ill at the idea of being in any kind of social situation. Public speaking, large social events, even a small, intimate gathering among a few people can cause alarm if they don't know anyone in that group nicely. It is more than sweaty palms and a heart that beats so far you think it's going to jump right out of your chest. Muscle tension, fatigue, breaking out in rashes, hyperventilating, cold hands, and feet.

An introvert might not necessarily have SAD. Likewise, it does not mean an extrovert will never experience what it is like to deal with SAD, either. Although the symptoms of social anxiety and shyness are often intertwined with one another, SAD is experienced at a more severe level. Those who experience SAD often try to avoid any form of social interaction because they find it extremely difficult to be around people, believing that other people are judging everything they do and every move they make to the point that they cannot cope with. The stress becomes way too much for them. But it is essential to establish here that not all introverts struggle with SAD, and extroverts may be dealing with SAD again. SAD is a condition that should be taken seriously. If left untreated, it could lead to unhealthy vices like substance abuse. It could also lead to depression and suicidal thoughts, and that is a dark path you don't want to allow yourself to travel down, especially when you're reluctant to open up about seeking help, to begin with. SAD is a severe mental condition, and depending on the severity, it could lead to drugs and alcohol as a coping mechanism to drown out the pain. At its worst, SAD can be life-threatening. SAD can make you do things that other people might not do. For example:

- **You won't believe you deserve to be happy**: for some reason, sad will have you convinced that you don't deserve to be happy (many other types of anxiety can make you feel this way too). It makes you believe you're not good enough to talk to other people, so you choose to isolate and retreat from social gatherings instead.

- **You can't form connections**: you find it difficult to connect to others because all you can think about are the worst things about yourself. Sad will bring your self-esteem and confidence to such low levels that you don't feel like having a conversation with anyone because you're convinced they are judging you or they dislike you from the start. It's not that you don't want to form these connections because you do. You're so terrified of being judged and ridiculed you would rather not say anything at all.

- **You might become hysterical at the idea of being embarrassed**: the idea of possibly being embarrassed in public is enough to make you hysterical. The very thought that you could find yourself in an embarrassing situation where you believe everyone will laugh at you is enough to trigger a full-on panic attack. You prefer to completely isolate yourself and stay away from others, even if it pains you to do it. You would instead do that than risk the possibility of an embarrassing ordeal. Depending on your condition's severity, some people experience a meltdown and start crying hysterically, even if nothing has happened yet. That is how strongly impacted someone with sad might be by the mere thought of possible embarrassment.

- **Excessive worry:** social situations can trigger a stream of worries that you find impossible to stop. These worries grow so big until they consume you. You become distressed when you feel insecure and out of place in social situations, which only magnifies your fears. Your worries become so magnified that you have difficulty interacting with strangers or anyone in general with whom you are not familiar. Your day and night worries keep you awake at night, affecting your moods and ability to feel fully rested. You worry before the event, worry during the event, and worry long after the event is over.

- **You struggle to speak**: when you start panicking in a social situation, you could lose your speaking ability. It is not uncommon for someone with sad to feel like their throat has tightened up. The anxiety that weighs on your mind can be challenging to find the right words to say, and so you prefer to avoid speaking altogether to avoid being judged by others. Those who experience social anxiety sometimes feel upset because their fear is irrational. Their fear does not make a lot of sense to many people, and not many people will be able to understand what they are going through, which is possibly one of the most frustrating things about living with social anxiety.

When experienced intense, SAD can lead to a complete inability to function in social situations. Some people have been known to display selective mutism, unable to speak even though they want to say something.

CHAPTER 7:

Recognize different styles of attachment and how they affect relationships

Understanding attachment style in therapy

The relation is helpful and essential for human interaction, but how a person interacts or communicates with others can be related positively and negatively to various facets of his life. Attachment types were identified as one of the earliest elements of the creation of a human. This indicates that problems relating to relationships and mental health disorders can be attributed to the forms of attachment developed during childhood and modified through interactions.

Type of relationships formed

According to Martin (2017), relationships can be measured based on three major attachment styles:

- **Healthy attachment** can build a solid, supportive relationship, where the person is confident to communicate their desires and emotionally intimate.

- **Resisting attachment:** a more solitary environment, while the person will spend a lot more time alone and resist contact, as the name implies before the interaction is too painful to drive others away.

- **Nervous attachments:** contradictions in relationships that may be demanded by the person but which are ignored at a time. These individuals are generally called sticking, but they do not have healthy relationships because of this discrepancy.

Martin (2017) adds that these types are created through interactions between parents and children and influence adult interactions. The variety of attachments that we make affects the human being and his self-confidence.

Description of events

An association is created because the caregivers are diligent and compliant with the individual's wishes. A good friendship with a partnership or other intimate interaction may do this in adulthood. These three imbalanced communication types are negative, concerned, and evasive. This happens whether the caregiver is withdrawn or irresponsive in childhood or prior relationships. This adds to an uncomfortable sensation anytime a friend attempts to be more vigilant. Finally, attachment forms arise when the caregiver becomes unreliable, nervous, and distressed. The person is unaware whether the affection is continuously there to be vulnerable and comfortable when being so far apart. They feel free from the expected dismissal.

Application to therapy

A specific interaction or interview may decide the form of commitment formed by the person concerning their perceptions of a partnership. You will choose how your communication style impacts your present relationships and the challenges following the life objectives. The childhood experiences related to the development of forms of attachment suggest mental health conditions, such as anxiety into adulthood, according to Schimmenti and Bifulco (2015). Knowing the style of the client's relationship helps the therapist tailor the treatment to the circumstances leading to these disorders' development. The attachment form's root is the critical source of effective counseling (Mikulincer, Shaver, Berant, 2013). If the heart of the attachment pattern can be established, the therapy cycle can ultimately be guided to the root of the inability to establish stable adult relationships. The practitioner must fully understand the various attachment styles, the assignment context of these styles, and the associated events assigned to these styles to help determine a customer's best course of treatment. Attachment may mainly be rendered through childhood, but different partnerships may have modified the attachment type from one area to another by the provision or non-provision of a stable attachment matrix. Therapy should be customized to produce optimal results for the patient. It is essential that the client feels confident in thinking about their connections and other familiar things that have altered their communication patterns. The therapist must establish a successful partnership with the practitioner. Approaching the beginning of relationship issues without understanding these attachment types will compromise the client's best result.

Do you understand the look of an established partnership between your customers?

Why attachment matters in adult relationships

The relationship between parent and child is defined in attachment theory by parents' willingness to react physically and emotionally to their child. The bond is described as stable or vulnerable based on the parent's ability to establish protection and how the child reacts.

A child must have faith in their parents to think that the relationship is a haven and that the world is a safe and stable environment. Children need to trust innately that their parent is there for them when they need them. I don't know many people who would argue that this is not the best way to raise all babies. This need for connectivity is innate in any human being. We don't seem to talk in adult relationships about attachment, but it is equally necessary. The passion in adult relationships is very different because it is mutual. A parent doesn't expect a sense of protection from their kids, but a partner certainly looks for that (even if they are unaware of it). Adults need to believe that a connection provides stability and protection to have a more in-depth, better expressed, better coherent, and optimistic sense of self and others. The fact that there is a sexual aspect is another distinction in adult relationships. Here too, we see how intimate the need for health and protection defines the sexual relationship between partners. "No defense, no sex" is a traditional refrain of adult intercourse. At the very heart of a marriage is the question, "Are you there for me? If I need you, to count on you to be there physically. Can I count on you to be there for me if I have an emotional need? Can I count on you to understand that my relationship demands protection and security so that I can reveal my true self? Will this protection allows me to explore the planet and find my place there?"

The sensitivity and openness of each partner to the other's emotional signals in relationships determine whether there is a sense of a stable foundation on which to travel. This sense of stability and safe connection is missing in strained ties. Isolating or disconnecting a parent or partner from an attachment source is painful, intrinsically. Emotional disconnection drives people into anxiety and uncertainty. The brain reads a partner's actions as "dangerous," and because of our hard work to survive, we take a posture of challenge, flight, or freeze.

Each activity responds in a mutual feedback loop by a partner. It looks at a couple all over in a destructive loop that may lead to the collapse of spouses' relationships. The greater the frustration and hopelessness in the relationship, the more reactive, linear, and self-intensive the emotional and behavioral responses between the spouses become. Couples are trapped in a destructive circle between repetitive attitudes and misunderstandings. Whenever a person struggles to respond in a moment of great need, a sense of fear and vulnerability develops until a few individuals get trapped in an assault loop and protect themselves over the moment. These loops are guided by rage, sadness, loneliness, shame, and terror.

Securely connected couples cannot go into a negative cycle as profoundly and can quickly exit either process. Such couples will convey precisely what disturbed or caused them. Partners can control their emotional pain through separation and can give simple, consistent signs of needs when reunited. Indeed, attached partners will support each other and embrace warmth and reassurance. Moments known as vulnerable or dangerous can be recognized and addressed. Couples should draw on their experience and construct a coherent, precise account of their relationship.

In short, securely attached pairs can address a potential deterioration without triggering a negative attack/retirement period. Couples tend to be more open and direct and also prefer to connect more to their friends. There is a stronger emphasis on individual needs and a broader sense of concern for the spouse. Communication is polite, as well as constructive. In reality, this is "successful dependency," the ability to feel connected to others and trust that they are autonomous.

CHAPTER 8:

Toxic relationships

Toxic/Abusive Relationships

Emotional Abuse
- Minimizing
- Humiliation
- Gas-lighting
- Violation of trust
- Neglect

Sexual Abuse
- Forcing, guilting into uncomfortable acts

Intimidation
- Using fear with looks, actions or behaviors
- Destroying property
- Displaying weapons

POWER & CONTROL

Psychological Abuse
- Threats made or carried out
- Mind games
- emotional blackmail and/or humiliation

Using Privledge
- 'Man of the house' mindset
- Having the last word
- Rigid male female roles

Isolation
- Controlling, limiting who she sees, what she does , or where she goes
- Keeping from friends and family

Anxiety isn't always the element that affects a relationship. Sometimes it's the other way around, and the reason you are afraid is because of a toxic relationship. But what exactly does poisonous mean? We refer to a toxic relationship when it isn't beneficial to you and it's harmful somehow. The building blocks for a healthy relationship are made from mutual respect and admiration, but sometimes it just isn't enough.

However, there is a difference between a problematic relationship and a toxic one, mainly the poisonous atmosphere surrounding you. This kind of relationship can suffocate you with time and prevent you from living a happy, productive life. Many factors lead to toxicity. It is most often caused by friction between two people who are opposites of each other. There is nothing specific to blame in others, and the toxic relationship grows out of a lack of communication, the establishment of boundaries, and the ability to agree on anything, or at least compromise.

Take note that not all toxic relationships develop because of the couple. Sometimes there is an outlier seeking to influence conflict because they will benefit from it somehow. This type of individual takes advantage of other people's insecurities and weaknesses or manipulates their way into a relationship they have something to gain. In some cases, a toxic person seeks to destroy a relationship to get closer to one of them. Personal needs, emotions, and goals take priority over anyone else's wellbeing.

With that in mind, let's briefly explore the characteristics of a toxic relationship:

- **Poisonous:** a relationship that is extremely unpleasant to be around as it poisons the atmosphere around it. It makes anyone around the couple anxious, and it can even lead to psychological and emotional problems, such as anxiety and depression.

- **Deadly:** toxic relationships are bad for your health. In many cases, it involved risky, destructive, and abusive behaviors. Some people end up harming themselves with alcohol, drugs, or worse. Injuries and even death can become the final result.

- **Negative:** in this kind of relationship, negativity is the norm. There is no positive reinforcement, even when children are involved. The overwhelming lack of approval and emotional support is standard.

- **Harmful:** toxic relationships lack balance and awareness. Those involved are never truly aware of each other and lack the most positive principles that a healthy relationship needs. Toxicity also promotes immoral and malicious acts that harm a romantic relationship.

While it is true that some of them are, that's not always the case. However, psychopaths are expert manipulators due to their ability to mask their true feelings and intentions. These people have a psychological disorder that makes their personalities imposing, pretentious, and even impulsive. Many aren't aware of their behavior and its effects on others. They tend to be self-absorbed and expect a great deal from others while being narcissistic and deceitful. In other words, they lack insight as well as empathy. Psychopaths are people who seek attention, admiration, and acceptance, but they will need to accept their responsibilities and the needs of others.

Why and how would anyone end up in a relationship with someone who displays psychopathic traits? The answer lies in their ability to maintain appearances and manipulate others. If they realize you see through their charade, they will do anything to convince you that they are the right person. They may start doing good deeds, not out of empathy and love, but out of the need to redeem themselves. These people can recover if their psychopathic disorder isn't too severe in many cases. With help, they can gain control over themselves and their toxic behavior to live a productive life without hurting others in the process.

As mentioned earlier, toxic relationships don't always involve psychopaths or those who display similar traits. In many situations, these relationships are the way they are due to decent people who are terrible decision-makers or lack social skills. Taking a wrong turn in life happens to everyone, and many people change, but not always for the better.

Warning signs

Now that you can better identify toxic relationships and the kind of people that are involved, let's see if you're in one or not. Humans are complex creatures, and the traits we discussed don't necessarily make someone toxic. Some underlying issues and disorders can make people behave negatively. However, they can still be excellent partners. With that said, here's a list of questions you can ask yourself to learn more about your relationship:

- How do you feel about the company of your partner?

- Do you feel happy, safe, and nurtured in the presence of your significant other?

- Are all the other people involved in your relationship safe and happy? For instance, your children (if you have any), parents, friends, and so on. As mentioned earlier, people tend to avoid toxic relationships instead of being in contact with them.

- Do you experience anxiety or panic attacks when you are about to discuss something with your partner?

- Is your partner pushing the limits of what you would consider ethical? Are they even crossing the line of what is legal?

- Does your partner push you to perform challenging tasks that you consider unnecessary? These challenges may seem pointless, and that you need to resolve them just because it's what your partner wants.

- Do you feel emotionally strained and exhausted after interacting with your partner?

If you can answer some of these questions positively, it can likely cause you anxiety and damage your health. You must then decide for yourself whether you want to stay in this type of relationship to repair it or you want to leave. If you decide to stay, you must make many decisions. For example, you have to resist all the negativity that comes with a toxic partner because you will need to endure feelings of anxiety and stress.

Handling a toxic relationship

As mentioned, a toxic relationship can be a powerful source of anxiety. It doesn't have to be a romantic relationship either. Some of them you can avoid by cutting contact with some people to feel relief. However, there are certain people you simply cannot break away from, whether they are romantic partners or your mother-in-law. This is why we are going to discuss how to deal with such a relationship.

The first step is to accept the inescapable situation. When your options are limited, you cannot achieve relief by avoidance, and acceptance decreases anxiety. You may be tempted to be hostile towards that person, but it won't help. Instead, it will just add to your worries and stress. At this point, your only alternative is managing your anxiety by admitting to yourself that you may never be able to get along with that person. Also, you can attempt to ignore them entirely by never spending time together and ignoring any contact. However, none of these tactics usually work.

Resistance can help short-term, but it will continue generating anxiety and stress because the toxic person knows how to get under your skin and take advantage of you. Accept that this relationship is complicated and challenges you, but you are doing your best to improve it. That doesn't mean you should completely surrender. Accepting your situation will allow you new possibilities and new options instead of repeatedly punishing yourself.

Take note that you need to be consciously aware that you are not responsible for anyone else's emotions and reactions for the process of acceptance to take hold. Toxic behavior often makes people blame you for their situation and feelings. Do not accept any of that, as you are not the reason for their suffering. They need to take responsibility for their thoughts and actions instead of blaming others.

The second step is telling the truth. If a toxic relationship creates stress, you often lie to avoid conflict, which causes even more anxiety. The problem is that when you lie to such a person, you enable them and become partially responsible for the reality they create—leading to the toxic environment surrounding them.

For instance, let's say you intentionally didn't invite the problematic person to your birthday. When confronted about it, you may be tempted to say that you sent an invitation but used the wrong address, or it went into the spam folder. Lying isn't easy, especially if you are an anxious person. People can tell, especially if you tend to make excuses for yourself often enough. Instead of lying, you should say the truth and the real truth.

This means that you shouldn't use an excuse. Just say they make you uncomfortable and too anxious; that is why you didn't invite them. Telling the truth can be difficult and even painful because it affects others. It takes a great deal of courage, and once you get through the experience, you will feel a powerful sense of relief. In the end, it's better to get something off your chest instead of carrying it.

CHAPTER 9:

Codependency

What is codependency?

In many normal relationships, we develop dependent relationships. This means that we prioritize our partners and rely on each other for love, and in times, we need support. The relationship is mutually beneficial, and neither person worries about expressing their true emotions. In a dependent relationship, both people can enjoy time spent away from the relationship while still meeting each other's needs.

However, in a codependent relationship, the codependent feels that their only value comes from being needed. They will make huge sacrifices, martyring themself out to ensure that the other person's needs are met. They only feel worthy if they can be needed. They exist solely for the relationship and feel as though they are worthless outside of that relationship. The relationship is their only identity, and they will cling to it at all costs, and within that relationship, they will ignore their own needs and wants, feeling as though they are unimportant. Someone with codependent tendencies will struggle to detach from their partner because their entire sense of self is wrapped up in aiding that other person. It may get so bad that it begins to impact the codependent's life negatively.

The codependent relationship can become all-consuming, taking over the person's life in all areas. Other connections can weaken and fail as the codependent focuses solely on the relationship with which the relationship is held. Career potential may be lost, or the codependent may be fired when the relationship interferes with the work quality. Everyday responsibilities may be neglected in favor of catering to the enabler, the person with whom the codependent is in a relationship. Overall, the entire relationship is built on the faulty ground and is dysfunctional.

Causes of codependency

Like NPD (Narcissistic Personality Disorder), many external factors are believed to cause a codependent personality to develop. This is because both codependency and narcissism are similar personality flaws stemming from the same root cause of damaged self-esteem.

Poor parental relationships

Often, people who have developed a codependent personality have grown up repeatedly having conflicts with their parents throughout childhood. Their parents may have prioritized themselves or somehow otherwise denied that the child's needs were critical. By often downplaying the child's needs, the child internalizes that those needs are not important enough to meet. After all, if the child's parents could not be bothered to tend to them, they must not matter. The child learns to prioritize his/her parents instead and feel greedy or as though a selfish decision was made when trying to commit to self-care. Oftentimes, this kind of relationship between parent and child happens because the parent has an addiction problem and would do anything to feed the addiction. The parent never matured past the selfish stage of development as a child and focused solely on him herself. Because of all the time spent focusing on the parent's needs, the child never develops the independence and identity necessary to be successful in life. Feeling incomplete when not needed, these people frequently seek out other enablers that will allow them to continue living in this fashion.

Living with someone dependent on care

When a child grows up around someone else who requires frequent or around-the-clock care beyond the realm of normal, whether due to severe illness, injury, or some sort of mental illness, the child's needs may go unmet in favor of meeting more pressing ones, as the child is pushed aside in favor of the person who needs the care, the idea of the child's needs becomes less important to become internalized. The child may also engage in some of the care for the dependent person as well, causing his needs to be put on the back burner as he takes care of the person who literally cannot care for herself. While living with a family member who requires extra care does not necessarily cause codependency to develop independently, and many people can make it through the caregiving stage without issue, certain circumstances.

It can become an issue with certain personality types that are predisposed to codependent tendencies. It becomes an issue in particular if the child is younger when there is someone dependent on care. The child's parent tends to focus entirely on the dependent instead of spending the time the child needs to grow and thrive meeting the child's needs.

Abuse

It is no surprise that abuse, regardless of physical, emotional, or sexual, leaves lasting harm on a child. While some children abuse others, others may fall into a pattern of codependency. A child exposed to repeated abuse eventually begins to develop a coping mechanism to suppress their feelings. They begin to ignore and cast aside the pain they feel due to the abuse, which ultimately teaches them to ignore their own needs later in life. This leaves her only caring about other people's needs while neglecting their own.

Victims of abuse also tend to look for people with similar tendencies to those of the abuser, which is familiar to them. They know how to live through the abuse and understand that the relationship will often revolve around codependent behaviors. Abusers and narcissists love codependents, as codependents will tolerate vast amounts of abuse that would make other people balk.

Key features of codependency

Often, codependency manifests in incredibly recognizable ways. Though every person is different, and the behaviors will change depending on the relationship, codependency has several behavioral patterns. Knowing how to identify these will enable you to recognize when you or someone you know is exhibiting codependent tendencies. If you feel as though you may be codependent, seeking a professional opinion from a trained psychologist would be a great place to start your journey toward understanding yourself.

- **An exaggerated sense of responsibility:** codependents frequently feel as though the weight of their loved one's actions is on their shoulders. They feel as though they are directly responsible for the actions of their partners, children, or anyone else with which they are codependent.

- **Sensitive when good deeds are unrecognized:** when a codependent feels her efforts have gone ignored, she is likely to feel hurt or as though she was not good enough. She will try to martyr herself to get the recognition she craves to soothe her low self-esteem and prove that she matters further.

- **Feeling guilty when caring for self:** any time the codependent engages in acts she may see as selfish or unnecessary in the grand scheme of things, she will feel guilty. After all, her needs should be met last, and if she does anything other than that, behaves selfishly, which is unacceptable to her.

- **Rigid:** codependents do not tolerate change. They often seek out familiar things for this reason, which leads them to continually seek out other enablers in relationships, even if those enablers prove to be abusive.

- **Cannot set healthy boundaries:** codependents see no boundaries between themselves and their enablers. They have no sense of self that is outside of the relationship or apart from the enabler. Because they fail to set boundaries, the relationship eventually consumes their lives and leaves little room for anything else. This lack of limits also leads to needs going unmet.

- **Needs recognition to feel whole:** without recognition for good deeds and caring for others, codependents feel unwanted and unimportant. They require people to recognize their actions to help bolster their fragile self-esteem.

- **Need to control others:** codependents, feeling utterly responsible for the actions of their enablers, also seek some level of control over the relationships. Because the codependents always do everything possible for the enablers, they develop that control they desire, and the enabler allows them to have it. Without control, the codependents feel unable to help.

CHAPTER 10:

Fear of abandonment

The overwhelming worry that the individuals close to you will leave is fear of abandonment.

Anyone can develop a fear of abandonment. It can be deeply rooted in a traumatic experience that you had in adulthood, a kid, or a distressing relationship. It can be nearly impossible to maintain healthy relationships if you fear abandonment. To avoid getting hurt, this paralyzing fear can lead you to wall yourself off or you might be sabotaging relationships inadvertently. Acknowledging why you feel this way is the first step in overcoming your fear. On your own or with therapy, you may be able to address your concerns.

Negative thoughts and how to eliminate them

Negative thinking can become a bad habit. Thoughts sink into the mind and stay there until you get rid of them by taking action.

It can be tempting to strive to force those thoughts out of your head when you think negatively. Try to make them disappear forever and expel them. This strategy, however, is often counterproductive.

By making things worse, fighting those negative thoughts can reinforce that thinking pattern. The more you strive not to think about something, the more you end up thinking about it. You have to try a different approach to getting rid of negative thoughts, which will aid you in clearing your mind once and for all. Seven ways to clear your mind from negative reviews are here.

1. **Modify body language:** to observe your body language, take a moment. Do you have a hunch or a closed posture? Are you frowning? If so, it will make you more likely to think negatively. Inappropriate body language can reduce your self-esteem and result in a lack of trust. It is natural to begin to have bad thoughts in that emotional state. You have to open up your posture and smile more to feel safe. Correct the language of your body, and you will feel much better. It might just be what you need to erase those negative thoughts.

2. **Talk about the topic:** negative thinking sometimes appears because there are issues or feelings you need to communicate. Keeping things to yourself is not good. You should not do it if something needs to be talked about. It shapes and makes them visible by putting thoughts into words, and that will help you put the issues in perspective so that you can deal with them more effectively.

3. **For a minute, try to empty your mind:** it is difficult to remain calm when your mind is running at fifty miles an hour. It is more difficult to control thoughts, especially negative ones, in this way. Often a minute of calm is sufficient. It can be beneficial to meditate, and you should think of it as a reboot. It can be filled with something a little more positive once the mind is empty.

4. **Change the focus of your reflections:** negative thinking is sometimes the product of a low perspective. Take a look at the point of view you take before the stuff around you happens. For instance, you may think, "i'm facing some challenges, but i'm working on finding solutions," instead of thinking, "i'm going through a difficult time, and i'm having problems." except that the second form has a more positive point of view, you say the same thing. That small change of focus can often make a big difference in your thinking patterns.

5. **Be innovative:** it is beneficial to find a creative outlet for those thoughts when negative thoughts arrive—things to write. Draw something or paint it. Through creativity, exploring feelings acts as self-therapy and will raise your mood. The imagination will feel like a release. You break the habitual dynamic of your thoughts when you process your emotions through a form of art or creativity, and it will be easier for you to understand and control them.

6. **Take a stroll:** it is easy and clear to assume that this is where they form because thoughts reside in the mind. That's only partially true, however. Our thoughts are a product of the environment sometimes. If you are surrounded by negative individuals, for instance, you are likely to start thinking negatively. Getting away from this negative atmosphere can help significantly. It could be enough to take a short walk with your head somewhere, like a park or a museum. The time you have from negative influences will give you a necessary space of calm.

7. **List everything in your life that is worthwhile:** did you forget all the good stuff around you? Sometimes we lose focus on the reasonably good things present in our lives, in the daily routine. To return to concentrate on all the good that is happening around you, you must train your mind. No matter how little they seem to be, list each of the things you should be grateful for. In this respect, do not take anything for granted. Sometimes, right in front of our faces are good things in our lives, and we still can't see them. Stop being blind to all the things you already have that are positive.

The style of the attack because it is dangerous

A sudden and intense moment of fear and anxiety is an anxiety attack. These anxiety attacks can sometimes occur unexpectedly for no apparent reason, but they can also be linked to specific triggers.

"Anxiety attack" is not a clinical, formal term. Instead, it is a term that many individuals often used colloquially to describe all kinds of anxious responses. People can use it to describe a variety of sensations, from concerns about an upcoming situation to intense feelings of fear that would satisfy the diagnostic criteria for a panic attack. Understanding the context in which the symptoms occur is vital to understand what someone means by "anxiety attack."

Where it comes from and how to win it

Many individuals are considering making resolutions to change for the better at the start of each New Year. Of those who manage to make resolutions, many fail. But many people fail because of fear before they give success a chance. Some are scared of failure, and others are scared of performance. This immobilizes too many, regardless of the source of the fear, and prevents them from achieving what they want and are capable of. There is no way of failing than of never trying. Do not let fear kill your hustle this year before you even get going. Here are 10 methods to overcome fear and make this year where you are held back by nothing.

1. **Comprehend fear and embrace it:** fear exists to keep us safe. It is not bad or good, but a tool to make better choices that we can use. Fear is not intended to keep us inactive, but to help us behave in ways that produce the outcomes we need and want. Embrace fear as guidance and let it inform, but not control, your actions.

2. **Stand there, don't just do something!** We tend to admire individuals who are quick to act, but actions also include being deliberate, creating a plan, and pacing yourself. Many a successful undertaking by haste alone has been threatened or ruined. When fear strikes, consider whether analyzing the options and making a wise, well-thought-out choice might be the right action rather than jumping to what seems right in the heat of the moment.

3. **Name that fear:** the mere act of expressing your fear sometimes gives you the strength to handle it. Say your fear out loud, note it down, or concentrate on it in your mind. It grows when you try to ignore your fear. It shrinks when you face it.

4. **Long-term thinking:** you might be afraid you won't make the next payroll if you're an entrepreneur. But what is your outlook for three months or the view for three years from now? Your short-term problem will not be fixed by thinking about the long term, but it can help you think about it better and develop the right solution.

5. **Just educate yourself:** we fear nothing more than the unknown. If your fear results from a lack of information, then instead of speculation, get the information or knowledge, you need to examine the situation based on facts.

6. **Prepare, practice, play roles:** in the united states, the long-standing top fear is public speaking. Death itself ranks second in many studies to standing in front of a group and opening your mouth. If your anxiety is aligned with your performance, then prepare, practice, and play a role in a particular activity. Dr. Jill bolte-taylor, more than 200 times, practiced her popular ted talk (more than 18 million views and counting). Gallo says, "i find it ideal for practicing a presentation at least 10 times if you don't have that much time."

7. **Utilize pressure from peers:** have you ever done something terrifying, like jumping off a high bridge into a river below, just because you were with friends egging you on? Depending on how it's wielded, peer pressure, like fear itself, can be positive or negative. Surround yourself with the people who will push you to overcome the fears that hold you back from what you want.

8. **Success visualization:** before achieving it, athletes may imagine completing physical tasks thousands of times. This mental mapping ensures that it's more likely to follow its pre-ordained path when the

body moves. The same practice will assist you in whatever you're trying to achieve.

9. **Gain a feeling of proportion.** How big of a deal is that thing you're afraid of? Sometimes we get so caught up in a particular quest's achievement or failure that we lose the sense of where it aligns with everything else we value. Ask yourself, what may be the worst thing that could happen? Sometimes the truth is bad, but sometimes you may find that the fear itself is worse than anything you're afraid of happening.

10. **Receive help.** Whatever you fear, is it something you have to do on your own? To help you through it, can you find a mentor or support group? Athletes have trainers. Students have educators. Sometimes friends can provide the needed support to face your fear, even if they have no expertise in the area you're struggling with.

CHAPTER 11:

Insecurity

Why am i so insecure? What causes insecurity?

There is an internal dialog that accompanies our feelings of comfort. This is called the "sensitive inner voice." The critical inner voice is created by traumatic early life encounters in which we have experienced or endured hurtful attitudes towards us or others close to us. We unconsciously embrace and perpetuate this negative behavior pattern towards ourselves and others when we grow up. So, what are the events or actions that form this inner critic? Our contact with our powerful early parents can be at the root of our vulnerability as adults. Picture a child yelling at a parent. "You're just spacing out! Can't you find out something on your own?" Also, consider the negative remarks and attitudes that parents convey towards themselves. "In this, I look bad. I'm so fat." Such behaviors don't even have to be verbalized to affect the child. Parents' absence will leave children to feel anxious and convinced that something is deeply wrong with them. An aggressive parent may lead children to become introverted or self-reliant in ways that make them feel insecure or untrustworthy of others. Studies have also shown that excessive praise can damage a child's self-esteem. The right mindset for parents to cultivate is to view themselves and their children honestly and treat them with respect and compassion. The perfect strategy for a parent to help their children is to encourage them to find something special to them—something that lights them up and strives to achieve. This behavior must be in the interests of the infant, not just the parents. As the author and civil rights activist, Howard

Thurman famously said, "Don't ask what the world needs. Tell yourself what makes you come alive and do it. And what the world needs is people who have come alive." While the child pursues whatever desire they have, the parent will support and appreciate the effort involved, rather than concentrating too hard on the result. It's the difference between saying, "What a beautiful picture. You're the greatest artist I've ever seen," and saying, "I love the way you've used so many colors. It's cool that you've worked so hard on it. How did you come up with this idea?" This method allows a child to develop a sense of self-worth.

The effect of insecurity

Many issues form our vital inner voice, from negative attitudes towards our parents' perspectives and ourselves towards themselves. When we get older, we internalize these points of view as our own. We hold these beliefs alive by trusting in our insecurities as we live our lives. Dr. Robert's and Lisa Firestone's most popular inner vital voices people feel during their day include:

- You're stupid.

- You are unattractive.

- You never do the right thing.

- You're not like the rest of the men.

- You are a loser.

- You are fat.

- You're never going to make friends.

- No one is ever going to love you.

- You will never be able to quit drinking (smoking, etc.).

- You're never going to do something consequential or special.

- What's the point of trying?

Like a mean coach, the voice tends to get louder as we reach our goals. "You're going to mess up any minute. Everyone is going to know what a disappointment you are. Just stop before it's too late." Sometimes, we respond to these thoughts before knowing that we have them. We can grow shy at a party, pull back from a relationship, project these in attacks on the people around us, or behave against a friend, partner, or child. Just envisage what life would be like if you didn't hear these thoughts—mean echoes in your mind. Imagine what life would look like if you could live independently from this prescribed fear.

Insecurity at work

Insecurity will affect us in various aspects of our lives. Each person may find that their inner critic is more outspoken in one field or another. For example, you can feel pretty comfortable at work but completely lost in your love life, or vice versa. You can also find that as one region changes, the other may deteriorate. Some of us can contribute to getting self-sabotaging thoughts about our future at one time or another. Old ideas that we are inept or that we will never be noticed or respected will drive our insecurities through the roof. Such rising inner critical voices regarding one's profession include:

- You don't know what you're doing here.

- Why do they want you to do it on your own?

- Who do you think you are? You're never going to be effective.

- You're under a lot of pressure. You can't take it with you.

- You're never going to get anything done. You're so lazy.

- You're always going to put this off until tomorrow.

- No one ever appreciates you.

- You're better off being subtle, or you're going to get killed.

- No one here likes you.

- Think of your job first. Don't take any time for yourself.

- When do you finally get a real job?

- No one should have recruited you.

Insecurity in relationships

Whether we're single, dating, or in a serious, long-term relationship, there are many ways our vital inner voice can slip into our romantic lives. Relationships, in particular, can give rise to past hurts and experiences. We can lift insecurities that we've buried for a long time and bring up feelings that we don't expect. Many of us harbor latent fears of intimacy. Getting close to someone else will shake us up and push the feelings and vital inner voices even closer to the surface. Listening to this inner critic will do significant harm to our interpersonal relationships. It can cause us to feel desperate for our mate or pull back when things start to get serious. We can exaggerate feelings of envy or possessiveness, or these feelings make us feel rejected and unworthy. Famous critical inner voices that we have against ourselves regarding relationships include:

- You can never find another person who understands you.

- Don't get too close to him/her.

- He/she just doesn't care for you.

- He/she is excessively perfect for you.

- It would be best if you kept them involved.

- On your own, you're better off.

- They will condemn you as soon as they get to know you.

- It would help if you were in charge.

- When they get angry, it's your fault.

- Don't be too weak, or you're only going to end up getting hurt.

Steps for overcoming insecurity and for regaining self-confidence

Do you still feel like you have all the potential in the world, but for one reason or another, are you still holding back? You have a vivid imagination, and you can see infinite possibilities.

There appears to be no target within your mind's eye out of control. Yet, for some reason, in the real world, you just can't seem to bring yourself to do all the stuff you're talking about. It's as if there's something that prevents you from enjoying life in an ideal way. So, what's that? What is this thing that prevents us from tapping into our full potential? Well, in truth, it's always not one thing but a multitude of things that come together to form the base of all our insecurities.

If we feel unsafe about something at that moment, we cannot fully trust ourselves. Without trust, there is no doubt. This leads to hesitating actions where we fail to take decisive steps towards the desired outcome. We prefer to struggle with extreme anxiety and fear because of our vulnerability. We avoid taking constructive steps and judge ourselves unfairly when our high expectations are not met. Although fraught with fear, we are building dangerous attachments to others. We use people as a forum to raise our self-esteem. We depend on them to construct our self-esteem. We secretly hope and pray that they will bring the best out of us. Yet time and time again, people have let us down, which only plunges us deeper into our vortex of vulnerability. But why is that? Why are we doing this to ourselves? You feel uneasy when you make irrational assumptions about yourself or your capacity to do something. Such interpretations derive from unrealistic assumptions that establish a false perception of how you or things will be in different circumstances. For example, you may expect perfection from yourself. The actual reality; however, is very different from the imagined reality. You obviously cannot live up to those kinds of standards, so you surrender to the fact that you're just not good enough. When you're feeling "not good enough," this leads to a lack of confidence.

You do just not trust yourself. You feel insecure and incapable of being yourself when you are with other people. You're concerned about being punished, rejected, or attacked. This anxiety prevents you from achieving your full potential. You're dealing with low self-esteem, and you can't live the life you want.

CHAPTER 12:

Negative thinking

Identify your programmed negative contemplations

To move away from the negative reasoning that keeps you away from having an uplifting standpoint, you'll have to turn out to be mindful of your 'programmed negative contemplations.' At the point when you remember them, you're in a situation to challenge them and provide them with their walking requests to move directly out of your head.

Challenge your negative considerations

Regardless of whether you have consumed a large portion of your time on earth thinking, contrarily, you don't need to keep being negative. Stop and assess whether the concept is valid or accurate at whatever point you have a negative idea, especially a programmed negative idea.

One approach to challenge negative contemplations is to be objective. Record the negative idea and consider how you would react if another person told you the idea. You could almost certainly offer a rejoinder to another person's cynicism, regardless of what you think is hard to accomplish for yourself.

Replace the negative considerations with positive contemplations

When you're feeling confident that you can spot and challenge negative considerations, you're prepared to settle on dynamic decisions by supplanting negative contemplations with positive ones. This doesn't imply that everything in your life will consistently be sure; it's not unexpected to have an assortment of feelings. Notwithstanding, you can work to supplant the everyday unhelpful speculation designs with musings that help you to thrive.

Minimize outside impacts that invigorate your pessimism

You may know that particular sorts of music, violent computer games, or motion pictures impact your general attitude. Try limiting your introduction to distress and invest more energy tuning into quiet music or perusing. Music benefits your brain truly well, and books on constructive reasoning can give great tips to being a more joyful individual.

Avoid 'high contrast thinking'

Thought also called 'polarization,' is all you experience. It either is, or it isn't; there is no nuance. This can lead individuals to feel just as they need to accomplish something impeccably or not at all.

To maintain a strategic distance from this sort of reasoning, grasp the shades of darkness throughout everyday life. Rather than intuition, as far as two results (one positive and one negative), make a rundown of the middle results' entirety to see that the things aren't as critical as they appear.

Avoid 'personalizing'

Personalizing is making the suspicion that you are at fault for whatever turns out badly. If you take this kind of speculation excessively far, you can get suspicious and feel that nobody likes you or needs to spend time with you and that every move you make will baffle someone.

Avoid 'catastrophizing'

This is the point where you accept that the most exceedingly awful and conceivable result will happen. Catastrophizing is typically identified with anxiety about performing inadequately. You can battle catastrophizing by being reasonable about the potential effects of a circumstance.

Visit a quiet spot

It can assist with having an individual departure when you have to turn your disposition around. Numerous individuals find that investing a little energy outside improves their mood.

If your working environment has an open-air region with seats or outdoor tables, plan a little personal time to be outside and revive yourself. If you can't genuinely visit an outside serene spot, have a go at meditating and visiting a wonderful open-air region with an ideal climate in your mind.

CHAPTER 13:

Too much jealousy

Is your spouse unreasonably jealous? Or is it someone in your marriage who feels jealous when your spouse focuses on other people or interests? Who can show such behavior? Jealousy of marriage is a poisonous emotion; when this emotion spreads too far, it will destroy the marriage.

However, if you have media influence and curiosity and are healthy in a jealous relationship, you may be affected, as shown in a movie or TV series.

Jealousy stems from insecurity. A jealous spouse does not feel "enough" for the partner. Their low self-esteem makes them see others as a threat to their relationship. In turn, they try to control their partner by preventing any friendship or hobbies they have with the outside world. This is not healthy behavior and will eventually make the marriage doomed.

Jealousy starts from childhood. When we call it "same level competition," we will observe it at the same level. At this age, children compete for the attention of their parents. The feeling of jealousy begins when the child thinks that he has not received his unique love. As children grow up and gain healthy self-esteem; this misconception will disappear most of the time.

But sometimes, this phenomenon still exists, and the green-eyed monster grows, eventually turning into a romantic relationship when the person starts dating.

Therefore, before studying how to stop jealousy and overcome jealousy in marriage, let us understand what causes jealousy and marriage insecurity.

What is the basis of jealousy?

The problem of jealousy begins with low self-esteem. Jealous people have no innate sense of worth. A jealous spouse may have unrealistic expectations for marriage. They may have grown up in the fantasy of marriage, thinking that married life is just like what they look at in magazines and movies.

They might think that "abandoning everyone else" also includes friendship and hobbies. Their expectations of what a relationship is are not realistic. They do not understand that each spouse must have its external interests to be suitable for the marriage.

Jealous spouses have a sense of ownership and possessiveness towards their partners and refuse to allow their partners to be free agents. They worry that this freedom will make them find "better people."

Causes of jealousy in marriage

There can be many reasons for being jealous of relationships. The feeling of jealousy may arise due to specific situations, but if it is not adequately resolved at the right time, it may continue to occur in other cases.

One of the key reasons for jealousy is unresolved childhood problems. The jealous spouse may have solved the competition problem at the same level. This kind of competition is even possible in groups of friends or peers. In addition to childhood problems, their previous experience in unfaithful or dishonest relationships was also wrong.

They believe that by being vigilant (jealous), the situation can be prevented from happening again. On the contrary, it caused insecurity in marriage.

They did not realize that this unreasonable behavior would harm the relationship and drive out their spouse, becoming a self-fulfilling prophecy.

The sickness of jealousy creates a situation that the sick person tries to avoid.

Pathological jealousy

A minimal amount of jealousy in marriage is healthy; most people say that when their partners talk about an old love or maintain innocent friendships with members of the opposite sex, they feel jealous. But excessive jealousy and insecurity in marriage are abnormal and may even lead to dangerous behaviors. For example, OJ Simpson is a jealous husband, and Oscar Pistorius is a jealous lover. Fortunately, this type of pathological jealousy is rare.

A jealous spouse is not only jealous of the partner's friendship. The objects of jealousy during the marriage may be working hours or indulging in weekend hobbies or sports.

In any case, the jealous person has no control over the situation and therefore feels threatened.

Yes, this is unreasonable. This is very harmful because the spouse can hardly assure the jealous partner that there is no threat "there."

How jealousy destroys relationships

There are too many jealousy and trust issues in marriage, even the best wedding because it permeates all aspects of the relationship. Jealous partners demand that we continue to ensure that the imagined threat is not real.

Jealous partners may take dishonest actions, such as installing a keylogger on their spouse's keyboard, hacking their email accounts, browsing their phones and reading text messages, or following them to see where they "really" went.

They may destroy their partner's friends, family, or colleagues. These behaviors have no place in healthy relationships. A spouse who is not jealous finds himself in a constant state of defense and must consider all measures taken when not with his spouse.

Is jealousy unknowable?

Dealing with jealousy in marriage requires a lot of time and energy. However, you can take appropriate measures to eliminate the deep roots of jealousy.

So, how to deal with jealousy in marriage? You can take many steps to prevent jealousy from interfering with your marriage. The first step is to communicate. You can try to make yourself full of trust in your relationship and make your spouse feel comfortable with the problems bothering them.

Also, if you feel that you have contributed to jealousy in your marriage, you must try every possible way to suppress your emotions. If your wedding is threatened, it is worth consulting to eliminate the source of jealousy.

Typical areas where a therapist will provide you with services include:

- Realize that jealousy hurts your marriage.

- Admit that the act of jealousy is not based on any facts that occurred in the marriage.

- Give up the need to control your spouse.

- Stop all spying and surveillance.

- Rebuild your sense of self-worth through self-care and therapeutic exercises, aiming to teach you to be safe, loved, and worthy.

Whether you suffer from unusual jealousy in your marriage or your spouse, we suggest you seek help when you want to save your marriage. Even if you think that marriage is no longer helpful, it is best to receive treatment to check and eliminate the source of this bad behavior. Any relationship you may have in the future can be a healthy relationship.

CHAPTER 14:

Importance of working on yourself

Sometimes it appears to be simpler to adore others than to cherish yourself. However, self-acknowledgment is an essential piece of building solid associations with others. Luckily, with a little arrangement and development, you can likewise figure out how to cherish yourself.

Forgive yourself not matter your past

A common obstacle to self-love is that we all used to have things we could not forgive. Maybe we feel sad about how we treat our ex. Or, we think that we are too short with our family because of depression or fatigue. Or maybe we have experienced months/years of losing streaks in our lives, which is not unforgivable.

Here are some things to do to forgive yourself:

1. **Focus on your feelings:** one of the first steps to understand how to forgive yourself is to focus on your feelings. You need to identify and process the emotions before you can move on. Give yourself permission to understand and acknowledge the feelings you have caused and embrace them.

2. Acknowledge your error aloud: when you make a mistake and keep struggling to let it go, acknowledge loudly what you've learned from the error. When you speak out the thoughts in your mind and your heart's feelings, you can be free from any of the pressures. You also cement what you have learned from your acts and the consequences on your memory.

3. Discuss with the own critic: journaling will help you consider your internal criticism and improve self-compassion. Pickell says one thing you should do is write a "conversation" with you and your inner critic. This will help you recognize patterns of thinking that sabotage your capacity to forgive yourself. You should also use your diary to make a list of the things you enjoy about yourself, including your strengths and talents. This will help boost your self-confidence when you believe you have made a mistake.

4. Show goodness and compassion to yourself: if your first reaction to a negative situation is to blame yourself, it's time to demonstrate some kindness and consideration. The best way to continue the path of forgiveness is to be loving and compassionate towards yourself. This takes effort, maturity, and a reminder to your person that you deserve forgiveness.

5. Spend time with yourself alone: whether you're unmarried, in a romantic relationship, or married, one of the easiest ways to maintain a loving relationship with yourself is to spend time alone daily. Irrespective of your introvert or extrovert status, everybody will benefit from some real-time alone.

6. Take yourself to an eatery: go by yourself to a movie. I am taking a long morning stroll. Lay on your bed and take a deep breath. Meditate for a couple of minutes in the evening. Whatever activity alone draws you to time, make it happen. When you allow yourself the time and room to listen to yourself simply, you might be surprised by what ideas and revelations pop up for you.

7. **Make sure you insert play into your daily activities:** the re-prioritization of play into my life is one of the most significant improvements i've begun to create in my life in the past year. I took a play inventory (aka i sat down with myself and demanded, "what did i do before life got so serious for fun?") and began to honor the responses that came to me. After this discovery, i've begun to take improved lessons, take more pictures, make more short videos, go skateboarding, and i've been heading to janet jackson's occasional dance class and dancing. If your very meaningful, very frustrating adult life has taken a backseat to play, then you will need to re-prioritize some stuff.

8. **Restrict the quantity of junk food that your brain consumes:** just as your body gets grumpy if you regularly feed it lousy stuff, so does your disposition suffer when you provide junk to your mind. Avoid watching the news. There's a fair possibility that the bulk of the information delivered to you is shitty, pointless, and fear-based, depending somewhat on which country you live in. Avoid eating such garbage to the best of your ability. Instead, consume only highly enriching information. Quit viewing 'reality tv.' i used to watch jersey shore. Then i quit because when i watched it, i felt gross. It doesn't help you to observe people evaluate their actions privately and feel superior to them. Unfollow or unfriend persons that just perpetuate hate and negativity through the social network newsfeed. I've got about four thousand facebook contacts. Still, i only subscribe to less than 40 of them. Just as you carefully examine the kind of food you ingest, you must be extra careful concerning the type of information, news, or gossip you expose yourself to. Both of them matter more than you feel they do.

9. **Sleep adequately well:** approximately a third of your time is spent on the bed sleeping, so you may as well be skillful at it. We may either be deprived and exhausted by the way we sleep, or it can invigorate and elevate us. Get some good quality blackout curtains, restrict some electronic light emission within 2 hours of going to sleep, and keep your bedroom free from any mobile phones/laptops/tvs. It's

time to cuddle or have sex when the lights go out, not update your instagram feed. Spend your time with specific things as your targets and be intentional. In your life, impose real restrictions to take time for the items that matter most to you. Say no to people with whom you do not want to share time. Say no to tasks at work that do not serve you and your core beliefs. Spend time daily among your favorite pals. Take out time and allow time for laughter, lightness, and playfulness in your year. The more you honor yourself, the more your inner child can feel heard, understood, and cherished with how you invest your time.

10. **Create time for relaxation:** you want to make sure you still give yourself the freedom and room to breathe and enjoy amongst all of your nutritious foods, optimized sleep patterns, and playfulness. When you feel like it, take naps. When you like them, treat yourself to spa services. Let yourself soak in the salt baths of epsom for an hour while you are in the mood. In the self-care/self-love journey, rest is crucial. Allow yourself to have no plans occasionally. Often, resting, laying down on the concrete, and just breathing is the only thing you can do for yourself.

11. **Keep your boundaries:** write down a list of things you need emotionally, important things that, if neglected or violated, annoy you or hurt your feelings. They may be, for example, to be listened to, getting sympathy when you are broken, to be celebrated when you succeed, receiving affection and tenderness without asking for it, being looked after, and to understand that everyone leans on you. For you, that is essential, and when someone violates what's valuable to you or crosses your lines when it hurts, you will know. Don't disregard that. Some thoughts tell you what is right and what is wrong. Let everyone around you know what the limits are, what you will accept, and what you will not allow. You can excuse them if they apologize. You ought to establish consequences if they do not or continue to ignore the boundaries and desires. For instance, if you tell your spouse that when you talk about something, you need him to hear you and understand your emotions; however, he continually

ignores you or advises you to get over it. You should proceed with suitable action, such as seeking somebody else to trust.

12. **Do care for yourself as well as you do for anyone:** it looks easy, but many of us just don't do this because we think we're greedy or that it's not necessary to have our own needs met. No, to think about yourself is not selfish. Compassion for oneself implies expressing empathy for your own and other emotions. With gentleness, concern, and consideration, handle yourself on how you would take your kids or your closest mate.

13. **Surprise yourself:** discover stuff out of your reach to say yes to, stuff that you usually wouldn't say yes to. It would also help you get to understand yourself as well. You may discover that you like things you have never seen or attempted before. Move away from your comfort zone to see what will happen (it's most definitely going to be positive!).

14. **Find something you love doing:** it's convenient when you're feeling down about yourself to get caught in a rut. Whether it's golfing, gardening, cooking, picking an activity, sport, or art that you love. Discover anything that you love to do—anything. The likelihood is that if you enjoy doing it, then you're pretty good at it, too,' says jamie katoff, lmt, a san francisco-based marital therapist. "when we're doing things, we enjoy—and doing it well—we go through a condition called 'flow,' which increases feelings of trust and overall satisfaction. Learning how to be more consistent in that condition can contribute to more vital self-love and self-esteem feelings."

CHAPTER 15:

Don't permit past trauma to ruin relationships (use them to improve future ones)

You don't need to be dominated by your fear, so don't give in! You're going to concentrate on using your relationship anxiety to develop in this guide. This is a real sign of progress when you can turn your struggles into becoming a stronger person and a better spouse. It may seem hard to keep the anxiety under control, but by now, you should also realize that it's not impossible. This will show you a little beacon of hope, as you can find the methods that work for you and how your fear does not always have to guide you.

Establish a deeper connection

There was undoubtedly a great deal to chat about when you first started dating your girlfriend. Usually, the early stage of every relationship is buzzing with conversation and the urge to make an effort to please each other. This honeymoon stage is something that all couples realize is temporary, but it doesn't have to vanish completely. Try not to lose interest in them, even though you already know more about your mate.

People can change and evolve, so you probably don't know everything about your partner.

Your relationship with each other is infinite. This is the individual with whom you have chosen to spend the rest of your life, so make sure you can always show them how much you care and how much you are fascinated by them. The relationship can very quickly become stale when couples lose this magic. Not all marriages ought to fizzle out just because you have long been together. If you want to be in a thriving relationship, you both need to make an effort for each other. It requires work that you must always be able to build on. Keep learning about what you need from your partner and think about new ways to provide them with that.

Spend quality time together

Think about what's important to your partner, from their interests to their passions. If you two can spend quality time together doing these things, it will bring you closer. Besides, you would have a greater understanding of who your partner is. It feels incredible to hear about what you love doing when someone cares, so give your partner this feeling whenever possible. Instead of stressing what your partner may be thinking or desiring, you will hear about what they want. This will provide you with some relief from your anxiety in relationships. The anxiety derives from a fear of the unknown, so it makes sense that you will feel better if you know exactly what your partner loves to do.

There's a fine line between bonding with your partner and pressuring yourself to do stuff you don't want. You may have variations in what each of you finds fun, but you will be able to get even closer when you can find those commonalities. Just because you're a couple doesn't mean you're obligated to do it all together.

Try new stuff because you want to, not because you like you need to push yourself to do it. This will show your partner that you are truly interested in doing things they enjoy without sacrificing your desires and passions. If you have difficulty seeking common ground, you can also look for brand new things that both of you have never done before. This way, exploring life will allow you to grow even closer to your partner. If you are both having fun in the process, it will cause your anxiety to subside. It is a very inspiring feeling when you can still find new and fun things to do with your significant other, mainly when you have already been dating for a while. Just because you are married or in a long-term relationship, life does not have to become dull. Having a sense of adventure would keep the magic alive. You will come together and find more things you both want to do when this happens. Couples sometimes forget that the exploration process does not end as the years' pass. There is no need for you to settle into a permanent routine. Being open to new experiences will keep you feeling refreshed while getting away provides you with a sense of security. You'll find that the more you try with your partner, the less anxiety you'll face about not being nice enough or exciting enough for them. You'll be taking action instead of succumbing to the anxiety that pops into your head. This will make you feel great and show your partner that the relationship is invested in you. It is less likely that couples who have fun together will get into fights about trivial things. You will both understand that you can do a lot more together to keep your connection healthy and keep your relationship feeling as it did in the beginning.

Go the extra mile

You can either be pushed to a breaking point by your anxiety or inspired to make a change. For instance, you should continuously think of new ways to show your partner love and affection without being clingy, as your anxiety may imply that you need to be. Do thoughtful and considerate things; focus on their wishes instead of smothering them. It can be an easy but successful way to show them how much you care by preparing a meal for your spouse or picking up their bedside table. While you are doing kind things for your partner, it is essential to be true to yourself. This is just as dangerous as letting the fear take over if you get to the point where you surrender your happiness to make your significant other happy. You need to find the right balance that makes sense in your relationship. Think of the little things you can do easily when you want to do something nice for your partner. Often, when you want to bring more effort into your relationship, less is enough. Make sure you're going on dates. It can be beneficial to your relationship to have a daily date night. Check out some new restaurants you've always wanted to try, spend a night exploring your place, or watch two back-to-back movies.

Without slipping into the same old habits you are used to, there are endless ways you can have a date with your partner. Know that these small items will add up instead of concentrating on the great things you want to do together. By integrating these tiny movements into your daily routines, you will take your relationship further than ever before. Let them know if anything reminds you of your partner. It can be very good to hear what your partner thinks about you when you are not together. It showcases your closeness and your connection. It's also a fantastic way to check in with each other and see how your days are going. Your aim ought to be to keep the romance alive. You should show that your relationship is much stronger than your fears, instead of fearing that the affair is already gone, as your anxiety leads you to believe. Tell yourself that what you have with your partner is exceptional, and do your best every day to cultivate it. Your fears will start listening to you when you can prove that you are adequate. Negative thinking can bring you very quickly into a very dark mindset. You may have a much-distorted view of your relationship before you know it.

It will serve as a reminder of why you should always try to keep enhancing your relationship by concentrating on the positive things you know you share with your partner. No one else but yourself will be able to convince you of this.

CHAPTER 16:

Learn how to listen

Developing your listening skills is probably the most crucial step to bridge the communication gap between you and your partner.

When people feel honestly heard, they feel empowered, loved, supported, and understood. We live in a busy world where people rarely have time to sit down and reflect on their feelings, let alone listen to someone else's. This is why it is imperative to develop your listening skills if you want your partner to feel loved and cared for.

But before we talk about something called "active listening," which is our goal, we need to show you the difference between really listening and pseudo-listening.

Pseudo-listening vs. Real listening

Pseudo-listening is a concept that we should all be aware of. As you may have guessed, pseudo-listening is only half-listening to what the other person says, not paying much attention.

One sign of pseudo-listening is when you start thinking about how to reply to what the other person is saying before they're done talking. Another is when you engage in other activities, such as looking at your phone when talking. This can lead to many issues since people who have this habit have trouble maintaining relationships.

They cannot fully process the information that other people share with them, which can be harmful to the relationship. Not feeling heard might also trigger anxiety in someone with fearful or preoccupied attachment styles. You need to make it a habit to listen, really listen to what other people say.

Listening blocks

Numerous things can hinder your capacity to remain focused on what the other person is trying to say to you. The vast majority of us have been in an icebreaker type of situation in class, at a retreat, or a meeting where everybody is required to stand up and say something about themself. Suppose you've even been in that situation yourself. In that case, you probably remember that your attention was mainly focused on what you were going to say about yourself rather than what other people were saying. Maybe you practiced your speech in your mind repeatedly to avoid making mistakes, or you were just too anxious about speaking publicly. Some people just have a short attention span and need to be doing many things at once.

Whatever the cause, listening blocks can only have a damaging effect on your relationship.

Active listening

If you feel that your communication skills require some work and improve your relationships, you should introduce active listening to your daily routine. Knowing about pseudo-listening and listening blocks is a good first step, but good communication requires additional work.

When you start to listen to other people truly, you will be able to respond more insightfully, in a way that makes them feel you fully support them. Everything from your words, actions, and body language will show that you are paying attention.

Next, we will talk about three techniques you can use to focus your attention on the other person and make them feel heard without judgment.

Step 1: paraphrasing

Paraphrasing is expressing the meaning of what someone else has said using different words. A practical example might help to make the concept clearer.

- **Person a:** i don't think my partner cares about me anymore. They never reply to my messages or calls anymore.

- **Person b:** so, you feel neglected because your partner isn't talking to you as often as they used to.

In paraphrasing, you use your own words to help you focus on what the other person is saying and to show that you understand the meaning they're trying to convey.

Everyone has different core beliefs and, therefore, different ways to communicate. Using paraphrasing, you will have more meaningful conversations because you're adopting the other person's words to your core beliefs using your own words. This can potentially eliminate any cognitive distortions and false assumptions.

Step 2: clarifying

Consider clarifying as an addition to paraphrasing. In this step, you will ask questions until you understand what the other person is communicating. Look at the example above once more. Notice how

Person B not only paraphrased Person A's statement but also turned it into a question? This is the idea behind clarification.

You will gather more information and know what message the other person conveys. This will also send a positive message to the speaker: they will see that you actively participate in the conversation.

Step 3: feedback

The third and final step is providing feedback. After you fully absorb and comprehend the information presented to you, it's time to share your thoughts. Once you have assimilated their words, you offer a message back, communicating that you have listened to the speaker and want to engage in a meaningful dialogue.

The key to providing meaningful feedback is to offer a message free of judgment. When the speaker receives positive feedback from you, they know that you understand their side of the story and feel empowered. This will also lead to less anxiety in the relationship. There are three basic rules you should follow when giving feedback. The feedback should be honest (even if it's painful); it should be immediate and have a supportive tone.

Sometimes people will share their problems with others to get them out of their chest and may not be looking for advice or feedback. Always make sure you ask the speaker if they want feedback before you provide it.

CHAPTER 17:

Master emotion

Emotions are a natural human phenomenon and are very present in pressing and painful times. Every day we are driven by some force of emotions:

- We take chances because we get excited about new opportunities.

- We cry because we are hurting and make sacrifices for those we love.

Those are just a couple of examples of emotions; they dictate our actions, intentions, and thoughts with authority to our rational minds. Emotions can become a real problem. When we act too quickly or act on the wrong emotions, we can make rash decisions.

Negative emotions, such as bitterness, envy, or rage, are the ones that tend to spiral out of control the most, mainly when triggered. It only takes one slip of our emotions to screw up the relationships in our lives.

If you have issues controlling your emotions, here are some steps that you can implement into your everyday life that will help you regain rationality, no matter what challenging situation you are facing:

Don't react right away

When reacting right away to these triggers, you will probably say and do things that you will later regret.

Before acting on emotions, take a deep breath to stabilize your impulses. Breathe deeply for just a couple of minutes, and you will be able to feel your heart rate return to normal. Once you become calmer, remind yourself that feeling this way is just temporary.

Find healthy outlets

Once you have managed your emotions, you need to learn how to release that build-up in the healthiest way possible; emotions are something that you should never let bottle up. Talk to someone you trust. Hearing their opinion of the matter can help to broaden your thoughts and regain control.

Many people keep a journal to write down how they feel. Others engage in exercise to discharge their emotions. Others meditate to return to their tranquil state. Whatever activity suits you, find it and use it when emotions get high.

Look at the bigger picture

All happenings in our bad and good serve a purpose in our lives. Being able to see past the moment strengthens your wisdom. You may not understand certain circumstances right away, but you will see the bigger picture as the pieces of the puzzle fall into order over time. Even when in an emotionally upsetting time, trust that there is a reason that you will comprehend in time.

Replace your thoughts

Negatively fueled emotions create negative recurring thoughts that make cycles of negative patterns over time. When confronted with these emotions, force them out of your mind and replace them with more positive thoughts. Visualize the ideal ending playing out or think about someone or something that makes you happy.

Forgive your triggers

Triggers could be the ones you love the most; your best friend(s), family, yourself, etc. Sometimes, when people do something that upsets you, you may suddenly feel angry, or when you recall that you could do other things in the past, you may feel a sense of self-disgust. This allows you to detach from your jealousy, fury, and resentment. As you forgive, you will discover that disassociating yourself from these feelings will do you the best.

We are bound to take the wrong action and feel the wrong things from time to time. To avoid acting out, simply take a few steps back and calm your spirit heightened from outside forces. You will be grateful for mastering your emotions when it comes to building and strengthening meaningful relationships.

Using the power of mini habits

Just after Christmas, in the days ending 2016, I was reflecting on the year. I realized that I had tons of room to improve but always failed at keeping up with my New Year's resolutions. Instead, I decided that in 2017, I would explore other options.

On 28 December, I made the choice that I wanted to get back in shape. Previously, I hardly, if ever, exercised and had consistent guilt about it. My goal was a 30-minute workout. Realistic, right?

I found myself unmotivated, tired, and the guilt made me feel worthless. The clear opposite of my 30-minute workout goal was chilling on the couch, stuffing my face with junk food, but my brain went to the idea of 'size.'

What if I just performed one push-up instead of carrying that guilty feeling around all the time? I know, right? How absurd of me to think that a single push-up would do anything to help me towards my goal.

I found a magical secret to unlocking my potential when I found myself struggling with my bigger goals; I gave in and did a push-up. Since I was already down on the floor, I did a few more. Once I performed a few, my muscles felt warmed up, and I decided to attempt a pull-up. As you can imagine, I did several more. Soon, I exercised for the entire 30-minutes!

What are mini habits?

Mini habits are just like they sound; you choose a habit you want to change, and you shrink them down to stupidly small tasks. For instance, if you want to start writing at least 1,000 words per day:

- Write 50 words per day.

- Read two pages of a book per day.

Easy, right? I could accomplish this in 10—20 minutes or so. You will find that once you start meeting these daily requirements, you will far exceed them faster than you would imagine.

What is more essential than your habits?

Habits are responsible for 45% of how we behave, making up the foundation of who we are and how happy we are in life.

People fail to change anything in their life, even the aspects they know need to change because they never instill new habits. Why? Simply because they have tried to do excessively much in the past, all at once. If establishing a new practice requires you to have more willpower than you can muster, you are bound to be unsuccessful. If a pattern requires less will, you are much more likely to succeed!

Benefits of mini habits

There are many other benefits of using small habits in daily life. Here are a few:

- Consistent success breeds more success.

- No more guilt.

- Stronger productivity.

- Formation of more positively impactful habits.

- Generation of motivation.

CHAPTER 18:

Self-care

L earning to love yourself fully and deeply might well be the essential part of the healing process.

I know changing your feelings on a deep level is a tall order. The challenge is made more challenging because we are so often besieged with messages of how "unlovable" we are. We believe we're not enough: that no one could truly love us, especially if they knew who we are.

Though the above statement can feel like the absolute truth at times, I promise it's total bullshit.

Every one of us is fully deserving of love. You are a human being who is not only allowed to love and be loved but who I believe was made to do just those things.

Grasping this is essential because it helps us to have a better sense of our self-worth. This ultimately leads us to stop needing external reassurance (or to need it a lot less), and it helps us learn to choose the right partners and seek relationships with people who will genuinely value us.

There are many ways to expand these practices, but I will tell you about what worked for me. Hopefully, these ideas can work for you, too, or provide a jumping-off point to discover what does work for you.

Take time for yourself: self-care

What does "self-care" even mean? It feels like a recently emerged, poorly defined buzzword.

When most of us envision "self-care," we probably think of a glass of wine and a steaming bath. Maybe we think of a day at the spa or something similarly relaxing.

These are excellent ways of caring for yourself, but they are far from the only methods of doing so. If you hate baths, rest assured, you can avoid the bubbles.

Self-care can take a variety of forms:

- Taking a walk in nature.

- Reading.

- Painting your nails.

- Watching a comforting tv show.

- Singing.

- Creating art.

- Cooking.

- Resting.

- Getting a massage.

Self-care, to me, simply boils down to taking time for yourself. Because only when we are genuinely alone can we dig deep to discover what's going on inside us. Spending time alone lets us know ourselves and connect with our innermost nature.

Not only is it emotionally and spiritually effective, but it invites us to learn to love ourselves. We learn to delight in our own company.

The importance of stillness

We need stillness: the chance to focus on our thoughts, feelings, sensations, and desires. There's a lot to be said for being still and "sitting with our thoughts."

Personally, it's something I struggle with a lot, and I'm continually working on embracing it. For me, sitting still is a fight. I feel restless and agitated, and relaxing seems to have the opposite effect. Nonetheless, I'm actively trying to incorporate more stillness in my life all the time. Learning to practice stillness will be an essential step in our journey toward healing from reassurance seeking.

We can think of self-care as falling into two kinds. The first kind is the more enjoyable one: self-care that emphasizes relaxation and leisure time. The second is the real "turning inward" that I'm talking about. It is often less enjoyable, but it's still necessary.

The two types of self-care can co-exist, occurring simultaneously and during the same activity. But to practice the second type, you must allow time and space for inward reflection.

It's so easy to block out our thoughts. For many of us, it is quite scary to be alone with them. I get that. Often, the last thing we anxious people feel like doing is focusing on our thoughts, giving them more room in our lives. They are numerous, and they are continually swirling around, tormenting us, surfacing forcefully and suddenly.

You're likely all too familiar with racing thoughts and constant worries. They're always there, and for reassurance-seekers, they are mostly present. They can be loud and invasive. The idea of sitting with your thoughts might seem overwhelming.

At first, it probably will be. Yet, paying attention to our thoughts is how we learn to quiet them. Instead of hiding from our intrusive (perhaps even obsessive) thoughts, we're going to learn to examine them, to question them, to turn them over in our minds, and to look deeper at what they're trying to tell us.

How does one practice be still?

The most obvious and familiar method is meditation. Meditation is an excellent tool as it helps you stay grounded and lets you examine what's going on inside you. The goal is clarity and peace. When your mind is clear, there's less room for the scary thoughts to come swirling around, and if they do, you can handle them far better.

Meditation can be straightforward. It can be brief, especially when you're just starting. Why not shoot for 5 minutes per day? Meditation also doesn't have to involve chanting mantras or anything fancy. The core of meditation is just sitting still and allowing your body and mind to relax.

I want to emphasize that meditation's goal is not to clear your head of thoughts entirely but rather to let them come and go. I encourage you to keep practicing and don't get frustrated if you keep getting distracted. Learning to meditate successfully is a journey that requires a lot of practice. Many great meditation apps can help you, too.

In addition to traditional meditation, practicing stillness can also take the form of prayer or going for a walk in nature. The important thing is to allow your mind to be calm, quiet, and open. This is when the real work can begin.

Journal effectively

Journaling can be an excellent healing tool, and it's so simple. You may wish to journal while in a meditative state or after embracing stillness, but you can also journal amid high anxiety. There is tremendous value in both approaches.

Journaling was beneficial to me on my journey away from constant reassurance seeking. You may have already noticed this, given how many journal excerpts.

I found journaling to be an all-in-one aid for my anxiety. It can take many forms, which is part of why it's a great tool. You can adapt it to your purposes and style. All approaches are valid, whether you prefer making lists, jotting down bullet points, or writing a stream-of-consciousness record of your thoughts. Research has shown repeatedly that there is real power in writing things down. Journaling gives us a way to release our thoughts, feelings, and worries.

We all need outlets to discharge our anxious energy and let our ideas flow. Often, letting the ideas emerge onto paper helps us see them for what they are: irrational and fueled by anxiety. It's funny how writing things down can help you know the truth about what's going on. This was very effective for me because it helped me become my own reassure. Instead of looking to Nathan for answers, I provided them for myself as best I could, which was important to me. It allowed me to slowly build trust in myself and reduce my need for external assurance.

Grant yourself grace

Here's another essential part of your healing process: give yourself grace. The journey we are on is not comfortable. If it were, it wouldn't require so much from us. But take heart: when things are tough, we often deal with the most worthwhile things.

Have patience with yourself during this time. (And at other times too!) Remind yourself that this is a journey, which means you will make progress and regress. That is okay. The road is choppy at times, and often, things get—or seem—worse before they get better.

When you stumble, don't beat yourself up. If you find yourself reverting to old anxious thinking and reassurance-seeking patterns, know that this is normal. You're working to alter practices that may have been established in you over years and years. Give yourself the grace you need. Be patient with yourself as you would a close friend. Give it time. Don't rush. This stuff is hard. You don't need to be "cured" just yet. You are on the path, and that is the most important thing.

Allow yourself to be loved

This will be one of the most challenging parts of the healing process for some of us. For many, relationship insecurity stems from deeply held beliefs about one's lovability. Are some of your fears based on a disbelief in your worthiness or ability to be loved? If so, it's no wonder that you seek reassurance. You don't have a firm understanding of your lovability, so of course, you're going to feel anxiety surrounding that. Welcome to my life!

CHAPTER 19:

Show empathy

What is empathy?

P eople tend to confuse empathy with sympathy. To have compassion for someone means to feel pity or sorrow for them when they face some misfortune. To have empathy means being able to understand and share their feelings.

It is not uncommon for people to disagree with each other on things. Everyone has their own opinions and feelings. However, it is essential to respect the other person's feelings and not railroad over them with your own. This is especially so in a relationship. You have to cultivate a sense of compassion and endure other people's views and emotions. Empathy will allow you to do this and develop a strong relationship with your partner.

Influence of empathy in a relationship

You need to have empathy for your partner, and they should do the same for you, too. For instance, you will understand their pain or feel happy when they are happy. If you can develop empathy within yourself, you will perceive your partner's emotions even as they keep changing. This is crucial in helping you understand each other and provide support when needed. Having empathy will help you become more compassionate. If you fail to empathize with the other person, you will not have compassion for them either. This is because you will fail to recognize their emotions and thus fail to react appropriately. According to many studies, people who lack empathy are usually the ones who are mean to others. They fail to understand how their words and actions affect the other person. Such people lie to themselves and refuse to take responsibility for their actions. They rarely show remorse for hurting another person. These days, people get so wrapped up in themselves that they neglect to develop empathy in their nature. This can hurt all their relationships in life, regardless of whether it is at work or home.

Empathy is actually at the heart of a happy relationship. Your relationship will struggle to survive when it lacks empathy. You will lack compassion without empathy, which will affect your bond with your partner. Empathy is like a bridge between two individuals who have different feelings, thoughts, or perspectives. Empathy can be of three types.

Cognitive empathy is when you can look at things from another person's perspective but cannot feel their emotions. It will allow you to appreciate a situation the other person is going through.

Emotional empathy allows you to feel what the other person is feeling or thinking. It will enable you to connect with the person more emotionally. Compassionate empathy is a balance of both cognitive and emotional empathy. It allows you to see things from the other person's perspective and empathize with their emotions.

Compassionate empathy is needed to develop to a greater extent within yourself. Cognitive or emotional empathy can often have a negative impact. For instance, someone can use it to manipulate someone for their benefit.

But with compassionate empathy, you will feel compassion and be less inclined to want to harm anyone. If you have human empathy, you will think twice before you do anything and be more considerate of your partner's feelings. If you know that your partner feels annoyed or frustrated when the room is messy, you will empathize and make an effort to keep it clean. Your empathy will help you become the right partner, and they will appreciate your efforts. Compassionate empathy will help you respond to your partner with love, compassion, and understanding.

How to develop empathy

Now that you recognize its importance, you should make an effort to nurture empathy within yourself. The following steps will help you to become more empathetic.

- **Increase your self-awareness.** When you become more attuned to your own emotions and thoughts, you will also recognize these in others. If something hurts you, you will know that it could hurt another person too. Take notice of how you feel and think when your partner says or does something. Don't be absorbed in yourself, and learn to exert control over how you react.

- **Practice self-empathy.** You will fail to empathize with your partner when you cannot sympathize with yourself. You need to pay attention to your own emotions and acknowledge when you are going through a difficult time. Don't compromise self-care in an attempt to take care of your partner. If you take care of yourself, you will be better able to care for them. You can face your issues without being catastrophic about them. Remaining calm and composed will help you meet everything that comes your way.

- **Pay attention to body language.** Be careful about your body language and learn to observe others as well. A person's gestures, expressions, and various movements can tell a lot about their feelings.

- **Observe nonverbal cues.** How a person says, something is often more revealing than what they are saying. The nonverbal cues will help to identify their emotional truth.

- **Develop the habit of listening well.** You won't empathize with someone if you don't even listen to what they are saying. Pay attention to the details and be a good listener. Avoid interrupting someone when they talk. Too many people are focused on talking more than listening. Give genuine attention to your partner at all times. Even when you argue, don't be focused on finding a way to defend yourself.

- **Look for the positive aspects of your partner and your relationship.** When you focus too much on the negative, you affect your ability to empathize healthily. Start taking note of the good things instead of always thinking of the bad.

- **Avoid being judgmental or doubting what the other person says.** Listen with an open heart and mind. Don't focus too much on giving advice or telling them what they should or should not do. When people share their problems, they trust you and look for support. It would help if you were more focused on listening than solving the problem. Keep your own opinions and values aside and focus on what the other person feels and needs from you. Being too entangled in your perspective will prevent you from acting mindfully toward your partner.

Use these tips to develop a sense of empathy for your partner and others. It will make a lot of difference in how you communicate with people, positively improving your relationships with them.

How to communicate with empathy

Acknowledge your partner's pain. You need to acknowledge how they feel at all times. They will feel supported when you connect with their struggle or pain.

You may use the following sentences:

- "I am sorry that you have to go through this."

- "i hate that this happened to you."

- "this must be hard for you."

- "i can see that this must be a difficult situation for you."

Share your feelings. You can be truthful and admit it when you don't know what to say or do. It is not always easy to imagine what the other person is going through. Share your thoughts and let your partner know that you are trying. You may use the following sentences:

- "I wish i could make things better."

- "i'm unfortunate that this happened to you."

Show your partner that you are grateful when they open up to you. People find it difficult to open up and be vulnerable to others. More often than not, their trust has been broken at some point. So, when they choose to trust you, you need to be grateful and express it. Show your partner you appreciate that they share their thoughts and emotions with you. You may use the following sentences:

- "I'm glad that you shared this with me."

- "i'm glad that you are telling me this."

- "i appreciate you trying to work hard on our relationship. I know you are trying, and that gives me hope."

Show your partner that you are interested. You have to take an interest in what your partner is going through. It can be hard to go through difficult times alone. You have to reach out and show them that you are there for support. Show them that you are interested in listening to whatever they have to say. Don't offer too much advice or too many opinions. Just be a good listener.

CHAPTER 20:

Exercises to improve yourself

A normal human response to stress is anxiety. Too much anxiety can interfere with living a safe, happy life. Try a few of the following exercises anytime and anywhere to find relaxation if you feel caught up in your anxiety. The aim is to execute activities that will help you relax quickly.

Relax by Breathing

You will also see that your heart rate and breathing are getting a little faster if you feel nervous. You might also begin to sweat and feel lightheaded or dizzy. Having your breathing under control will calm both your body and mind when you're nervous. Take these steps to get your breathing under control when you're anxious:

1. Sit down in a quiet and relaxed place. Place your chest in one of your hands and your stomach in the other. Your stomach can shift faster than your chest when you breathe in deeply.

2. Take a slow breath through your nose. Monitor and feel your hands as you inhale. Although the hand on your stomach will move slightly, the hand on your chest should remain.

3. Breath out slowly through your mouth.

4. Repeat this process at least ten times or until you start to experience a drop in your anxiety.

Relax by Visualization

Have you ever used the phrase 'seeking your happy place?' In reality, painting a mental image of a location that makes you feel comfortable will calm your brain and body.

Sit in a quiet and relaxed position when you start to feel nervous. Think of your dream spot to relax. While it can be any real or imaginary location in the world, it should be an image that you find relaxing, happy, quiet, and safe. Make sure that it's easy enough to think about it so that you can return to it in your mind when you feel nervous in the future.

Think of all the tiny things you would notice if you were there. Think about the smell, feel, and sound of the place. Imagine yourself in that spot, happily enjoying it.

Close your eyes and take long and frequent breaths through your nose and out of your mouth once you have a clear vision of your sunny spot. Be mindful of your breathing, and once you feel your fear lifting, continue to concentrate on the position you've pictured in your mind. Whenever you feel nervous, visit this location in your mind.

Have the Muscles Relaxed

You could experience pressure or stress in your muscles when you feel anxious. This muscle tension will make it more difficult to control your anxiety now you think it. You will generally decrease your anxiety levels by relieving the tension in your muscles. In moments of fear, to quickly alleviate the muscle tension:

1. Sit down in a quiet and relaxed place. Close your eyes and concentrate on breathing. Breathe into your nose and out of your mouth slowly.

2. To make a tight fist, use your hand. Tightly squeeze your hand.

3. For a couple of seconds, hold your clenched palm. Note in your hand all the stress you experience.

4. Turn your fingers open slowly, and be mindful of how you feel. A sensation of stress can be found, leaving your body. Your hand will feel lighter and more comfortable finally.

5. Continue to tense your hands, legs, shoulders, or feet, and then release different muscle groups in your body. You will want to work your way up and down your body to other tense groups of muscles. In any part of your body where you are injured or in pain, stop tensing the muscles, which may further aggravate the injury.

Relax by Counting

Counting is an easy way for your anxiety to be relieved. Find a quiet and relaxing place to sit when you sense anxiety running over you. Close your eyes and count towards ten slowly. Repeat and count to 20 or an even higher number if appropriate. Continue to count until you find it as the anxiety subsides.

This relief happens quickly sometimes, but other times it could take a while. Keep patient and relaxed. Counting will calm you because, aside from your anxiety, it gives you something to concentrate on. It's a perfect technique to use in a crowded or busy space like a store or train, where it may be more challenging to do other anxiety exercises.

Relax by holding yourself present

As mentioned earlier, mindfulness is the practice, kindly and without judgment, of being present in your current state and environment. When you feel your thoughts spinning and anxiety rising, remaining present will help you establish a relaxed state of mind.

To get yourself into the present outside of your thoughts:

1. Find a nice and quiet place to sit and close your eyes.

2. Note how it feels in your breathing and body.

3. Now, transfer your focus to the sensations in the world you experience. Only ask yourself what's going on outside of your body? In your area, note what you hear, smell, and feel.

4. Move your mind from your body to your surroundings multiple times and back again until your anxiety begins to fade.

5. Relax by disrupting your nervous thoughts

When you are feeling nervous, it can be challenging to think clearly. Anxious thinking can also make us believe that negative thoughts are real or do things that worsen our anxiety. Breaking or interrupting your anxious thoughts may be beneficial to think better and respond to your reviews appropriately. Here's how to break the loop of your nervous thinking: ask yourself if the constant concern is an issue for you. It's nice to be conscious of that if the answer is yes.

Try various ways to disrupt the nervous process of thinking, such as:

- Sing a silly song to an upbeat tempo about your anxiety, or talk in a funny voice about your anxieties.

- Pick a pleasant thought instead of your fear of concentrating on it. This could be a person you love, your place of happiness, or even something you're looking forward to doing later that day, like having a nice dinner.

- Listen to music or read a novel. Be aware when you move your attention from your anxiety to the task at hand and note how you feel.

- Relaxation is an ability that you acquire. It takes practice, just like physical exercise. Choose an exercise for anxiety and pursue it before you feel less nervous. Try a different one if one exercise doesn't work.

CHAPTER 21:

Avoid that anxiety in relationship influence other aspects of life

More than a relationship, anxiety is the most challenging problem to accept. We are always getting surrounded by this tension and stress. This feeling would decide our fate. We are all scared of it, but we can't run away from it because there will be no peace without facing the problem. Our surroundings will bother us with this situation and the feeling we have in our head about every little thing.

The best time when we should face anxiety is now. But how? Relationship is the most complex situation, which will make you more anxious about yourself and your life. Many reasons can cause anxiety, but the most common one is the relationship.

A relationship can be evaluated as the best and the worst experience of life. It makes us feel so dirty that we don't want that feeling anymore, and it also gives us so much happiness that we would like to get this every day. The relationship is an example of our life. It teaches us how we should behave with other people and how to love others unconditionally.

It is painful when anxiety comes into our lives, but this pain can be taken as a lesson. The world becomes more difficult with this situation, and the only thing that keeps us going is our passion, hoping that everything will be fine in the ending.

A relationship is a situation where we learn how to act and adapt to our surroundings. This is the best place for all those who are looking for a partner. It does not require much money or any qualification, but it requires so much communication and understanding from you.

Starting a new relationship is the best feeling; no relation would make us feel so good unless we start something new in life, which can change our whole being with little steps. But when something wrong happens, and you get into an argument with someone, it is then the time of real anxiety.

In the initial stage of any relationship, we are so lucky, but what makes us unlucky is that we don't know how to handle these situations. We all know that many relationships have ended just because of an argument. This is because they could not handle the situation with patience.

Anxiety is something that we can't run away from because it is a basic problem in our lives. Anxiety kills our joy. It makes us feel so worthless and unworthy that we don't want to live anymore. We get nervous about everything, and it makes us behave abnormally.

This stress doesn't only affect our happiness but also affects the quality of our life and health. People are getting sick because of anxiety. They don't get good sleep, and their eating habit becomes irregular, too.

There are hundreds of ways to prevent anxiety because we all have different kinds of nerves in our bodies. There are so many psychological solutions that can help us deal with the situation, but nothing works unless we accept its presence and try to understand it.

Understanding is the only way to make us feel better about our life. We should recognize that this feeling is also a part of our lives, and it should not be taken as an enemy. If we understand the feeling, then we can come out of this situation.

You should remember that there will be misunderstandings in every relationship, but it is not possible if you have not communicated when it ends. If you are facing anxiety in your relationship, then the best way to deal with this problem is by communicating with your partner or anyone with you.

Communication is the only way to get rid of anxiety because there will be no security without communication between two hearts. If you are ready to share your inner feelings, you can easily get out of the situation and find a way out.

You and your partner should be ready to face every situation that comes into your life. It is not that easy to go through this situation, but everything will be useless if you can't handle it. Break up is not the solution for this problem, so don't decide until you feel like taking something.

Anxiety is not a death sentence; it only allows us to learn about ourselves. It forces us to understand the value of time and brings us closer to each other. If you have decided to start a new relationship, then there will be problems, but you must solve these problems with patience; otherwise, nothing will work out for you in life.

CHAPTER 22:

The importance of communication

Regardless of whether it is a relationship with your better half or even your friends, there will be some challenges. Different factors are essential for the success of a partnership or even a long-term relationship. However, a necessary element of all is communication. The lack of proper communication skills can effectively ruin any relationship you have in life with anyone. It is quite vital to effectively and efficiently communicate what you want, need, feel, or desire with your partner for your relationship's health. The lack of proper communication often creates misunderstandings and feelings of resentment. These things can quickly ruin your relationship. The good news is that you can also improve your communication skills with any other gift in life.

General tips for better communication

Active listening

There is a difference between hearing what the other person says and actively listening to them. At times, you might even listen to what your partner says, but you may not be fully present while doing so. You might be distracted by something else or react to any strong emotions they display. In regular conversations, and especially during any heated discussions, you might impatiently wait to express your thoughts or wait for your chance of a rebuttal. You might be impatiently thinking about all the various ways in which you can respond to them while they are still speaking instead of actively soaking up what they are saying and then responding after. When you do this, you do not pay much attention to what your partner says because you're engrossed in your thoughts.

Now, with any talk about the concept of being an active listener, you must make a conscious effort to slow down your thoughts and listen to what your partner is saying, not just with an open mind but an open heart as well. Like most things in life, this is easier said than done. However, your intention is what matters, so this will be a starting point. If for some reason, you don't have the concentration to listen actively and openly to what others say, then you can put the argument or conversation on hold until after. Another simple way to become an active listener is by sharing your feedback. You merely need to restate or paraphrase whatever your partner says toward the end of the conversation to demonstrate the fact that you have been listening to what they were saying.

The conversation dynamic can shift positively when your partner knows they are being seen and heard. That said, I'm not suggesting you have to agree with everything they say, but you can effectively improve the communication in your favor by showing that you understand them. Even if you sound a little transparent while doing this, it is okay. At least you are making an effort to get started. For instance, you can say something like, "... did I understand this correctly?" Or "it seems like you are upset with me for not doing..."

As with any other skill in life, you can become an active listener, but it takes time and effort. You cannot develop the skill without practice, so start practicing your skills of becoming an active listener. The more you get, the better you will be, and the easier it will be for you. During an initial couple of weeks, active listening might not come naturally to you, but you will get the hang of it after a while.

Open-ended questions

"Do you ever stop talking and ever listen?" or "I wonder if you will ever clean up without me asking?" You might have used such rhetorical questions with your partner at some point or other. Well, do these seem like great conversation starters to you? I'm sure even you would agree that this is not the best way to start a healthy conversation or a dialogue. Sure, when you are frustrated, upset, or annoyed, these might seem like pretty good things to say in that instance. However, for the health of your relationship, these are good for you in the long run. You are essentially putting your partner on the defensive once again by making such statements or asking such questions. Once this happens, the scope for healthy discussion goes down the drain. Instead of transferring any unpleasant emotion into the conversation, start using open-ended questions. For instance, if you are unhappy that your partner doesn't clean up, try using an open-ended question instead of the rhetorical question mentioned above.

Instead of saying, "I wonder if you will ever clean up without me asking!" you can say something like, "I could certainly use more help around the house. What can we do about it?" or "It would be nice to get this all cleaned up quickly. What can we do?"

Internal editing

While you are communicating with your partner, you must make a conscious effort to avoid resorting to any form of personal criticism. It means you must refrain from displaying criticism either verbally or through your body language. So, don't resort to any putdowns, insults, negative criticism, or indicate undesirable body language, such as eye-rolling or dramatic sighs. The minute you start being critical of your partner, you immediately shift into the defensive. Once your partner gets defensive, whatever the topic of conversation was, it is most likely to turn into an argument or a nasty fight. When you put your partner on the defensive, it significantly harms the entire conversation. It not only limits how much you listen, but also the conversation will escalate out of anger, and you might both end up hurting each other with the things you say.

Keep calm

Whenever you are engrossed in a discussion with your partner, ensure that you keep calm. If you stay calm, the chances of a conversation spiraling out of control and turning into a massive argument will decrease. If you want, you can break from the conversation and then revisit the issue when you feel more emotionally stable and calm. Not just you; encourage your partner to do the same as well. It is better to discuss when you and your partner are emotionally stable and not volatile. You must also become conscious of any internal self-talk in your mind while conversing with your partner. For example, let's suppose you are in disagreement. Does your internal self-talk increase your ability to calm yourself down, or does it make you even more irritated? If you notice that this internal self-talk seems to be fueling the fires of emotional distress, it is time to change it. While in the middle of an argument, if you catch yourself thinking, "the last time we fought, the things they said hurt me," or "this is what they always do, and it is unfair," then stop yourself immediately. Engaging in negative self-talk will only worsen the situation at hand. Instead, don't do this and try to replace all this with calmness. Once you are calm and no longer seeing red, you are better positioned to express yourself and understand your partner.

Work on self-soothing whenever you are upset. For instance, maybe you can go for a short walk or even take a timeout and physically remove yourself from the room your partner is in. This helps ensure that your emotions are in check and you're the one in control of them. A conversation will be quite productive when your emotions are balanced, and your mind is clear.

Being gentle

If a problem bothers you, you can freely state the reason. While doing this, you must be gentle with your partner. Don't blame your partner, but instead, talk about what you feel and have experienced. When communicating questions, please pay attention to the tone used. Using a mutually respectful manner, you can start a constructive dialogue and open up communication lines between you both. Keep in mind that the style you use must not be aggressive or passive. Once again, if your partner detects any hints of criticism or passive-aggressiveness, the entire conversation will come to a startling halt.

Incorporate "i" statements

The best way to own your feelings while communicating with your partner is by using "I" statements. Instead of pointing out your partner's mistakes, concentrate on expressing how you feel because of their actions. The most common phrases you can start using are "I feel," "I want," or "I need." For instance, saying something like, "I feel bad that you said ____." By doing this, you effectively prevent your partner from becoming defensive while expressing yourself. It will also make your partner more self-aware of their behavior. This technique also encourages you to express yourself, your thoughts, and your emotions more clearly.

Perspective

Your perspective essentially determines everything you feel and think. For instance, you might say that the glass is half-empty, while your partner says the glass is half full. No matter what you think, the amount of water or any liquid in the mirror will remain the same. So, why not believe this is true from your partner's perspective. After all, the juice content is the same, and your partner isn't wrong. Placing yourself and your partner's shoes in any situation makes it easier for you to view things from their perspective.

Once you understand where they're coming from and why they are saying what they say, it becomes easier to understand them. It can also trigger feelings of empathy for you. The extent to which your relationship can be successful depends on whether you can accept influence from your partner or not. At times, all it takes is a mere shift in perspective to resolve a dispute.

Understanding

We all want to be understood, but one thing we all fail to do is understand others. You must first try to understand what the other person says before you demand that you are understood. You can use this simple technique while engaging in conversations with your partner, family members, friends, colleagues, or pretty much anyone in your life. It is an inherent tendency or desire to be understood by others as human beings. Take a moment and think about all the times you've said, "No one understands me," or "You don't understand what I'm trying to say!" For a healthy, loving, and successful relationship, you and your partner must understand each other. For a moment, don't emphasize your need to be understood, and instead, shift the focus to understand them better. This simple shift in how you use your attention helps clear a path for fresh communication and positively shifts the relationship's dynamic.

CHAPTER 23:

Understand conflicts

There will be contradictions in your relationships as long as you get involved with each other romantically. Some people claim that confrontation is bad for the relationship and would eventually lead to the relationship's destruction. Others argue that anxiety is beneficial for their relationship and will allow it to thrive. Conflict in a relationship may be both positive and negative. It could benefit as well as hinder the relationship. There is often tension in various situations, whatever state the relationship is in, and whether the relationship is being supported or harmed. There are also several explanations for conflict. Such causes include the absence of interpersonal communication skills, low confidence, physical violence, the experience of an individual in relationships, etc.

Not many in the world can tell you that they have a romantic relationship that is 100% successful. That can be illustrated by the high divorce rate in the United States. Nonetheless, for many years, some couples have been together. Because I am certain that conflict was a significant factor in the failure of several partnerships, I am also sure that good connections had a fair share of the conflict. In this paper, I have made nine suggestions that deal with such behaviors within romantic relationships. These are specified, summarized, and supported following the research available.

Thousands of women in the United States are sadly raped every day. The violence can be either physical, verbal, or emotional. By their definition, women seem to have a stronger sense of personal interest when engaged in a relationship. Women are taught to be a woman by society from birth to adhere to certain standards and meanings. When women grow up, here people still say, "That's not like a lady" or "You're going to be treated like a lady." What does being a lady mean? According to most cultures, women are the weakest and always need a man to look after them. Men are taught how to be a man from birth. Typically, this concept is dominant and regulated. This is reflected in phrases like "I'm the houseman."

If women are oppressed early in life or abused, it could set the course for anxious tendencies in their lives. Sexual abuse is an integral part of a larger social gender structure. The violence in these relations creates feelings of inferiority that are compatible with their childhood social learning. This violence creates emotions of inferiority and guilt, contributing to a sense of duty to maintain the relationship as much as possible. The majority of women in these situations gave up before giving up on their husbands.

When they give themselves up, they will eventually see violence as a social norm and expect it to happen in future interactions, thus repeating the processing repeatedly. Again, abuse is characterized as physical, verbal, or psychological in this context. As in any situation, the greater the exposure of an individual to a particular item, the greater the risk. In this case, women with more sexual partners are more likely to be close to the one who is involved in a kind of abusive behavior. With increased exposure to several intimate partners, there is a decreased sense of control for the women involved in these relationships. If a person loses control, they become weak and prone to violence.

In all dimensions of the concept, the case of violence with many partners has advanced, yet the highest degree of sexual violence occurs now. The ABI also recorded that 5% of female graduates have over seven sexual partners over six months. The highest incidence of violence in these relationships was found in this category. I think that anyone who exposes himself to such a large number would put himself in a position where the violence is required of an external observer. Dependence is described as an individual's dependence on someone else to fulfill their needs. In this case, the insecurity can be described as related to the relationship in which an individual has doubts and uncertainty. Insecurity is a sign that, in life, a person lacks a sense of need. Therefore, insecurity would be the counterpart of dependency, as an individual would then lack something depending on something else. This explains how "Theory" considers the number and significance of the needs that the relationship meets for the individual and the degree to which certain requirements are not satisfied by alternative means because of dependence on a given relationship. A greater degree of dependency may occur when a person assumes that a relationship meets specific needs and lacks alternatives to satisfying those needs.

The presence of another person who seems to be attracted to or perceived lack of interest by the partner involves multiple factors contributing to insecurity. Regardless of the cause of uncertainty, it still seems that this relationship is more based. The explanation for this is the assumption that the partnership will be broken and that the counterpart will preserve the partnership better.

For the relationship to thrive, proximity in any relationship is crucial. I agree that most romantic people feel this way and want this proximity. Nonetheless, I suggest that women see this proximity as playing much more of a role than men. As mentioned in the first proposal, men and women are taught about their gender roles when they are raised. Females are "supposed" to care for ties, and men are "supposed" to be self-employed jackers and hunters, who do not always have to be so close.

Regarding the proximity of romantic relationships, the spouse who is more likely to engage with others about problems that affect the relationship is the one who puts greater importance on proximity. Instead, such interactions are more likely to be avoided by the partner, who respects strongly less. 37 out of 72 interviewed couples reported differences of opinion as they discussed closeness and distance topics in a study by Judith Feeney. It does not necessarily indicate that the proximity was more significant for these women than for the men. As an interview said:

At least most of her life, she didn't even seem to want me. That is why I continued to respond by neglecting her because I hate being neglected. When I wanted to find flaws in her so I could feel better. With her, I always tried to find flaws. This man thought that closeness to the relationship was more important than his girlfriend. Despite his view on proximity, 26 out of 37 men who mentioned different concepts regarding proximity and distance said that the woman had a greater sense of proximity than the man did in their romantic relationship.

Every thriving relationship must be founded on trust. When you don't trust your partner or vice versa, the courtship or family will never have a stable base to be a success. Distrust of a partner's emotions forms an interpersonal division between the two partners. This obstacle would inevitably be the relationship's subject and therefore avoid all possibilities to concentrate on other things.

For example, if a man distrusts his girlfriend or spouse, he's always wondering if he is happy. She just tells him that she is happy and doesn't understand why he always asks. It is more than an annoyance for her, and she ends up telling him to stop asking. The man assumes that she's crazy and distrusts her feelings. This example illustrates how the emphasis moves from the relationship to the continued lack of confidence in its feelings.

Jealousy is one of the strongest and most dangerous feelings in intimate relationships when coping with conflict. Celestialism may cause depression, distrust, and/or angry relationships, which are all highly dangerous. When a person in a relationship has low self-esteem in one area of his life, they feel inadequate. The individual's insufficiency causes them to believe that their partner will get anything or something that they can't give from anyone.

There is also a possibility that the other half of this connection is overwhelmed by the daunting sensation that their partner is receiving something that it perceives as something they can't give out of the context outside of its partnership when their partner is worried about anything else (e.g., a future employer, work or a new friend). Both inside them and within the relationship, these feelings can cause tension.

Anxiety is often considered an unpleasant feeling that arises due to long periods of stress (Smeltzer and Bare, 2000). According to a study carried out in Britain, more than 800,000 Britons now have to "act in fear" and suffer from anxiety relative to that of 1993, and increase the overall number of suffering figures to more than 7,000,000. The economic burden of anxiety disorder, 1999, indicates that anxiety is invested annually at about $42 million. In reality, anxiety exists as a 'natural part' of our lives, influencing almost all aspects of our lives, including everyday activities, relationships, and entertainment. Fear affects the mind and the body, and we all want to free and escape from it.

But in some situations, some anxiety is useful and even indispensable (Eisold, 2011). Anxiety is increasingly becoming one of the most common mental disorders, with positive and bad points affecting several different generations around the world. This book, therefore, addresses three major components of the causes of anxiety and effective therapies.

Naturally, anxiety can be caused by two major factors, internal and external factors.

Internal factors

One of the obvious reasons that make people nervous is attitude. Personality is considered a characteristic of thought, attitude, belief, and psychology. He also states that combining various components such as linear thought, perfectionism, or high imaginative and imagined abilities contributes to "hyper-anxiety forms of personalities."

Specifically, people with these characteristics may be at greater risk of anxiety development. When certain people know that anxiety can generate results or help people gain more experience, anxiety is known to be a personality type. Personality, therefore, plays an important role in anxiety production. It is believed.

Indeed, individuals with these characteristics may be at elevated risk of anxiety. In certain situations, when people realize that anxiety can yield results or enable people to gain more experience, anxiety is considered a personality type. Personality, therefore, plays an important role in anxiety development. Many choices and expert research indicate that anxiety is usually inherited. Anxiety is true. If a person has nervous symptoms, they may experience the same one more likely.

External factors

Several factors in our daily life trigger anxiety-like job stress, financial problems, serious illness, or substance abuse.

There are also claims that if this status is suffered for a very long time before stress reaches its height, it may become anxious. An internal shift and anxiety are generated when one of the events in humanity, like circumstances, goals, or demands, is interrupted. In summary, people in modern society are easily nervous and are dissatisfied in all respects.

CHAPTER 24:

Express your point of view and understand the other

Preferred coping strategy

I f you find yourself worrying about the relationship, your best bet is to work on the issue together. If you have a conflict of opinions on something, try to find common ground by discussing the issue from both points of view and considering the other person's viewpoint. The other person may not appreciate being told you are right, and they are wrong. Sometimes a change in perspective or a different point of view can be helpful, so go ahead and offer this.

Behavioral experiments to test out specific fears

Behavioral experiments are really important for both people in any relationship to accept and understand each other correctly without jumping to conclusions that result from anxiety and worry.

Here is a sample list of possible tests to help you clarify your point of view from different perspectives:

- If my partner gets angry about something, i need to make sure that they will be ok.

- If my partner gets angry about something, i need to consider their feelings.

- If my partner gets angry about something and feels hurt, that must mean i can do nothing right. This must mean our relationship is headed for a downfall.

Behavioral experiments can be used to challenge each statement, such as the following: If you think carefully and realistically about such statements, you may very well find evidence that contradicts them.

You can even use behavioral experiments to gauge your reactions. For example, if you find yourself thinking, "If my partner gets angry about something and feels hurt, that must mean I can do nothing right," you can do a behavioral experiment to test out the thought. The experiment might be something like this: You might ask your partner to talk about their point of view on a topic. Let's say how tired you both have been lately. You listen carefully and take it all in and keep an open mind and an open heart. Then, when your partner leaves the room, you mindfully observe your feelings. Are you feeling hurt, bad about yourself, or ashamed? How do you feel after they leave the room? What is the effect on your attitude and thinking of having disagreed with your partner and being able to talk through it constructively? You can even journal about it afterward.

Practice talking about what's bothering you

Another big issue in being open with your partner is that it takes practice. Some people like to write letters or email them to their partners. It can be difficult for some people to talk about their worries with their partners, even if they love them very much. When they can talk about their worries constructively, it strengthens their bond. The couple can go over their differences and talk about them in a loving, kind way.

If you find yourself thinking that if you don't bring up the issue, your partner will never know. Take a step back. Perhaps it might be better not to talk about it at this time. It's helpful to trust that your partner loves you and wants what's best for you. When their point of view is different from yours, they probably have their reasons for thinking the way they do. This is why the "both sides approach" is important; it balances the relationship. If you find yourself thinking about something that bothers you repeatedly, it might mean it's been bothering you for a long time and that something deeper needs to be addressed.

CHAPTER 25:

Improve communication to perceive interest and be in the best of way with others

We want to communicate with people as it makes us cheerful—good contact is the secret to healthy social engagement. Yet what leads to a balanced conversation? Why stop over communication? Also, how can communication be improved in a relationship, a romantic one?

Communication importance

We are still so much in search of connection and belonging. That's why successful social experiences improve our emotional comfort and offer greater happiness in life.

It's the human experiences making life worth living. Social interactions in nursing improve satisfaction as sharing time with colleagues or friends produces optimistic emotions—a core aspect of satisfaction.

Interactions with individuals may be non-verbal or verbal—we may also communicate with a smile. Effective contact is also a critical aspect of successful social engagement. Still, what does this mean?

What is healthy communication?

A contact model typically requires a sender, recipient, and a message (nonverbal or verbal) that the sender encodes and the receiver decodes. It also requires input, the receiver's reaction to the noise, and post, interrupting contacts. Encoding relates to translating the sender's emotions into communicable texts.

The receiver decodes the message they receive—both nonverbal and verbal parts. While in principle, this sounds straightforward because you might assume a lot is occurring between them, and no message can be decoded without discrimination.

The way a document is decoded rarely becomes empirical truth. We also have our filters and expressive designs that render the planet's picture as we view it. What makes the correspondence cycle much more complicated is the reality that the sender's response is not ever purely truthful knowledge. We're about asking ourselves what our thinking is and Speech is an integral part of thinking.

Every message has 4 facets to it:

- **Fact:** what was informed about (statements, data, and facts).

- **Self-revealing:** what was revealed about me (info related to the sender).

- **Relationship:** what was my thinking about you (info regarding getting along how).

- **Appeal:** what was wanted by me in making you do something (attempting to control the receiver).

There's rarely the exact emphasis on every one of the 4 aspects, and the focus may be equally intended and understood. E.g., a woman who says, "empty is the sugar jar," might have less of the reality that there's no left sugar inside a jar and more of an urge for her spouse to go for the jar filling. To make things much more interesting, as receivers, we seem to be especially well qualified in one of the 4 "heads" (relationship ear, factual ear, appeal ear, or self-revelation). And if the spouse has a fine ear-relationship, he may decipher the statement to be like "you're incompetent because you've failed to fill the jar of the sugar," and he may retort like, "Well, you're not trustworthy, you've still not replaced the kitchen lamp!" Do you realize conversations like this? Things quickly unravel when we're not listening to one another. The fundamental emphasis on both the receiver and the sender's four facets will build an obstacle to safe contact.

It's necessary to realize that what we experience may not be what the partner intended to convey. Think of it: which is the best "head" you've developed? Are you, for starters, likely to hear some appeal in any sentence? And do you still feel challenged (hence, listen to your "brain" relationship)? We ought to be mindful of the 4 facets to get interested in good conversation. But go back to the original assertion; the next time you feel puzzled, just talk of the four dimensions. Where else do you perceive the message? Reflect on the real conversation details and use queries to explain whether you have missed what the partner was attempting to inform you.

CHAPTER 26:

Exercises to improve communication skills

Relationships rely on communication. Communication is, in many ways, the literal life-blood of the relationship. If you cannot communicate with your partner, the relationship will not build up trust, which is a huge problem for it. Thankfully, these four exercises can help you begin to communicate better with your partner. You will want to make sure that you and your partner know everything you are talking about, so you will better communicate and relate to each other.

Honesty hour

The first exercise is known as honesty hour. Ideally, you would have this weekly so you and your partner can communicate everything you have to say to the other person—judgment-free. If you cannot manage once a week, let it happen no less frequently than once a month. However, the important part about this is that you and your partner must agree that you will not feel offended about whatever the other person says. You must recognize that you and the other person are trying to communicate as clearly as possible.

With the agreement in place that neither of you will be offended or hold a grudge about what they have heard in this session, you and your partner will then sit down. For one hour, you both have the option to speak, freely, and without regard to anything but how you feel. This is not a time to hurt each other—do not call each other names. Do not tell each other that you hate each other. Simply take the time that you need to stop, sit down, and interact with each other. It would help if you listened while your partner talks—really listen to how they feel about your relationship right that moment. You must listen clearly and be free from judgment. If you can do that, your partner should do the same for you when it is your turn. Keep in mind that you cannot get defensive during this. You are not defending yourself here—you are getting insight into what the other person is saying.

"I feel" communication methods

The next exercise is meant to be used in arguments. While no one ever really wants to fight or argue, the unfortunate truth is that sometimes we do. It is just a fact of life—sometimes, there are arguments to be had. Sometimes, people feel hurt. Sometimes, we want to tell the other person that what they did is bothering us, and we do not know how to do so. The best way to approach these situations is always to voice our grievances in a very specific pattern.

The pattern here is that you will always say, "I feel..." instead of "You make me..." the idea here is that you are not going to be using any of those "your" statements that will automatically put the other person on guard. You must ensure that you are making it about yourself and talking about your feelings, which are subjective and, quite frankly, none of your partner's responsibility. It is not your partner's job to make you feel one way or another, and because of that, you must own that you have that control over your own emotions. Own your feelings. Stick to "I feel" statements to avoid causing problems in your relationship that you will not be able to easily or readily fix. This will go a long way if you can implement it regularly into your relationship and stick to it.

High and low nighttime chat

This next exercise is all about communication during the evening. You and your partner are going to check in with each other essentially. The idea will be that each of you will share the best and the worst parts of your day with each other, so you will be able to understand. It could be that these are points about each other, or it could be about something at work. Either way, the idea is that you will both be taking that time to communicate with each other so you will be able to better deal with each other.

When you do this, try to do so before bed, when the day is done. You will then ask each other about the best parts of your day. It could be anything—it could be the feeling that you felt when you saw a beautiful rainbow or the taste of the food that you got at the restaurant. It could be just about anything—all that matters are that you recognize each other's feelings about it. Similarly, you will then share the lows as well. The idea here is to be able to empathize with each other. How did what happened to make you feel? How is that good or bad? Is there something you can do to help with that low point? The idea will be that if you are the problem, or your partner is your problem, you can work together to fix it.

Repeating the other person's point

This exercise is designed to help you begin to understand the other person's perspective better. The idea is that, after you have finished listening to your partner, perhaps during one of those honesty hours, or even just during general arguments with each other, before you answer each other, you must take that time to stop, identify each other's feelings, and then recognize how you will be able to feel about each other. You will essentially be taking the time and energy to ensure that you and your partner are listening.

After one person has finished speaking, the other person must then paraphrase w what was said. After you finish paraphrasing the point, you will ask to ensure that your clarification of what is going on is correct. If it is, you will be able to then really think about your answer to the problem. After you have taken that time to understand the other person, you can then acknowledge how that makes you feel and vice versa. If you did not get it right, you could now ask for clarification to ensure that you are both on the same page with whatever is happening between the two of you.

CHAPTER 27:

What to do when you can't understand each other

Being in a relationship with someone with anxiety disorder problems can be stressful. Sometimes it can sound like fear; someone who wobbles between you and your friend is a third person in the relationship. This person always sows doubts and uncertainty.

Nobody has prepared you for it, and you cannot choose for whom you fall. There are no high school dating classes, let alone how to meet someone who has a mental illness.

Nonetheless, there is no need for anxiety to ruin the relationship or make it difficult to enjoy. You can love each other more deeply by understanding fear in general and how it affects both your partner and your relationship. Education can also relieve a great deal of stress.

The book breaks down all you need to learn and do when someone is anxious to talk about: how to help your partner, how anxiety can impact your relationship, searching for your mental health, and more. Keep reading if you want to ensure that your partnership does not become a third person.

Anxiety-filled conversation

If you ask or deduce it after monthly meetings, there will be a point when your partner discloses that they have to deal with fear. It is a critical time in the relationship, therefore be sensitive and do not judge. Thank you for trusting me with this knowledge, which you probably did not share with many people. See it as the start of a conversation that you can often resurface.

Understanding anxiety and knowing what it is doing to your partner

Learning fear and what your partner is doing will help you understand and assist the partner with some basic anxiety facts. Psychologist Dave Carbonell, Ph.D. psychiatrist Dr. Helen Odessky, among others, suggested bearing these in mind:

- Anxiety is normal. Everybody's got it. It becomes a problem or disorder only if it is serious.

- Anxiety is a real problem, not a composite. It's a problem in mental health.

- Anxiety can be a crippling condition that prevents people from working and living a normal life.

- Anxiety causes people to experience flight, battle responses, and worry about life-threatening issues, including whether a partner may cheat or leave.

- You can't "cure" or "fix" anxiety.

- Many people who have anxiety disorder wish they never had it. They are concerned that their anxiety is a burden for others.

- Millions of people have great relationships and are happy despite dealing with anxiety.

- Symptoms of anxiety, consistently or both may occur in waves. People with anxiety disorders or problems can have periods with no symptoms.

- Anxiety is not rational or logical. This causes people to worry about something, although there is no evidence that it is worth worrying about. It also causes them to act irrationally sometimes. Your partner probably knows that.

- Anxiety is not a weakness.

- Anxiety can be treated. Psychotherapy can alleviate symptoms and teach people how to treat them better.

How anxiety may affect your relationship

When you are dealing with someone nervous, your partner probably spends a lot of time worrying and ruminating about everything that may go wrong or already go wrong. Listed below are some examples of thoughts and questions in the brain:

- What if it doesn't love me as much as i do?

- What if it is hiding something from me?

- What if it lies to me?

- What if it cheats on me?

- What if it likes someone else better?

- What if we break up?

- What if it ghosts on me?

- What if it doesn't respond to my messages?

- What if anxiety ruins our relationship?

- What if i am only the first to reach out?

Most people have some of these worrying thoughts, at least. They are a normal part of a relationship, particularly a new one. However, people with anxiety problems or an anxiety disorder tend to have this anxiety more frequently and more intensely.

"Our thoughts are taking over and heading straight into the worst-case scenario," said Michelene Wasil, a therapist who understands both personal and psychiatric anxiety.

Anxiety causes physiological effects, including shortness of breath, sleeplessness, and anxiety. Anxious people can react to stress with the fight-or-flight response as if stress were a physical attack. Sometimes distressing thoughts motivate your partner to act in ways that stress and stress the relationship. For example, psychologist Jennifer B. Rhodes said, people with anxiety often check their partner's involvement with unsure approaches. These strategies usually address one of their anxious convictions.

Let us say that your partner is anxious to be the first to initiate communication. You don't like them as much as they want you to; they begin to worry because you do not send the first text as often as they do. Anxiety intensifies, and they start to think that you could never talk with them if they did not reach out first.

They agree that it's a good idea to fantasize about you for a while to cure this fear. This forces you to communicate first. Perhaps a couple of times, you'll touch them before they feel good, knowing you'd make an effort. The proof encourages them to doubt their unreasonable and nervous conviction that you will not hit first. Though, it's not a good approach.

Unfortunately, there are many behaviors in relationships motivated by anxiety. Here are a few more examples:

- Being controlling.

- Perfectionism.

- Passive-aggressive behavior or being avoidant.

- Being overly critical.

- Being irritable and angry.

- Having difficulty focusing and being distracted.

In case you are in a relationship with someone with a social anxiety issue, the anxiety is likely to affect your social life, preventing or exhibiting offensive behavior

Perfectionism meeting

You may not be able to bring your partner to all the social events or meetings you want to attend. Like other types of anxiety, this may give rise to disagreements or cause you two to grow apart.

How to deal with it

Anxiety doesn't have to jeopardize your relationship. You can have a healthy relationship through the right coping strategies and avoid anxiety by creating too much tension.

Encourage your friend to meet with a therapist. When you look after someone, you are tempted to support it by acting as a surgeon. The problem is that you are not a therapist. It will be emotionally draining to play that part. It could make your partner resent you.

You are not liable for your partner's counseling. That is why the partner should be carefully directed to meet with a therapist. A therapist can help them improve their treatment of anxiety in and out of a relationship. If you have a serious, long-term relationship, seek therapy for couples. Some problems of anxiety can depend on your relationship.

Meeting with a couple of counselors will relieve your partner from the strain. Instead of pushing them to do something for themselves, you encourage them to take part in counseling.

If your partner accepts or resists your suggestion to go to treatment, you should do it yourself. This helps you develop the skills needed to understand and deal with your partner's anxiety. A therapist can also teach you how to support your anxious partner more effectively.

It's easy to forget to take care of yourself if you meet someone with anxiety. You can always reflect on your mental health by going to therapy.

Learning how to communicate better about anxiety

Anxiety can be frightening. You should make sure you don't think about it. However, one of the most effective ways to deal with anxiety in a relationship is to talk to your partner openly, honestly, and directly about it.

"It is crucial to have candid talks together about what they feel and to validate those feelings," says therapist Daryl Cioffi. You need to encourage your partner to open up to show their anxiety. Try to listen, stand up for yourself, or take your fear personally.

Managing your reaction to relationship anxiety

It is easy to take it seriously and get angry when your partner talks about their fears in your relationship. Anxiety can be easily understood as egoism, denial, or a desire to separate itself said therapist Michael Hilgers.

"You're going to want them to get over it," said Hilgers. "You'd like them not to think about it." You can turn this ineffective default response into something more positive by practicing your coping skills. Here is an example to help you practice: assume your partner is afraid that she will betray you. When you take this seriously, maybe you think that she has this insecurity because she hates you or because she thinks you're the kind who would cheat.

As soon as you do it, you can begin to feel frustrated. You might respond defensively and say something meaningful.

"You will only worsen the problem if you can't bend without bullying," said Hilgers. Then you're going to strike again. Skip forward one hour later, and you fight. The point is bubbling. Perhaps you don't even know why you fight. Instead of making the tension rush up, take a moment to relax. Note that most likely, the fear isn't about you. You're not the source. It's your partner.

Ask respectfully what your partner feels. Something like, "I'm so sorry you feel like this. That must be tough. Can we do anything to help you feel more confident about that?"

"It's more important to manage your reactions than to manage your partner," said Talkspace therapist Marci Payne. It can help you be there and set boundaries for your partner. If your partner's fear causes you to freak out every time you bring it up, it will not help you.

CHAPTER 28:

Anger control during discussions

An individual's powerlessness to oversee their displeasure can end up being an extremely crippling character problem. Outrage has its down-to-earth incentive regarding why people have such a feeling. In any case, uncontrolled displeasure and fury can have various genuine ramifications for the individual exhibiting such conduct. When an individual is inclined to outrage effectively, the individual will have an extremely troublesome time overseeing his conduct. This can prompt various issues with others and make keeping up close-to-home connections very troublesome.

Likewise, the powerlessness for somebody to control outrage can demonstrate riskily. Blowing at some unacceptable individual can prompt a savage encounter. Such a circumstance can be gained out of power in a brief timeframe. Overall, it is only from a self-protection viewpoint to deal with one's indignation.

The initial phase in having the option to deal with one's resentment is frequently focused on getting to the displeasure base. Various individuals have outrage issues for various reasons. For a few, such indignation is established in confidence issues. Others are experiencing pressure and tension. At that point, some show such conduct because of subdued recollections that exist in the psyche mind. Despite the explanation behind the displeasure, one needs to acknowledge the genuine reason for the outrage issues. Thusly, it gets conceivable to keep the issue from compounding or turning wild. By recognizing the reason for the indignation, steps can be taken to control such upheavals. Frequently, such distinguishing proof alone is everything necessary for compelling indignation among the executives.

Realizing the displeasure's underlying driver can likewise permit you to get the moderate consumption of your outrage before it arrives at an upheaval level. Most exceptionally fierce and unstable furious upheavals result from an abundance of outrage growing gradually after some time. The weight fabricates and works until it discharges itself as an upheaval. Getting yourself right off the bat in the structure stages will permit you to make a couple of strides back and hinder the structure cycle. This keeps the perilous and fierce upheavals from happening, which is absolutely a strong method for outrage the board.

At the point when you first begin seeing that your displeasure is building, it might be wise to partake in a movement that can keep such pressure from arriving at minimum amount levels. Some may hit a punching sack to work off the strain, and others may just participate in a stroll around the square. The key is to recognize the structure pressure and afterward participate in something that guides in easing the strain. While this won't dispose of the entirety of one's resentment, it will surely lessen it largely.

Legitimate control of one's resentment can prompt a steadier life, which is engaging. What's more, it is certainly more engaging than being shackled to irate upheavals.

Taking an anger management class

Do you need resentment for the board class? Is it safe to say that you are continually shouting and hollering, failing to feel any harmony and calm in your life? If so, this kind of class could be the ideal response for you. Prevent such displeasure from controlling your life today.

With a class where you can learn approaches to control that outrage, you will find that life can be fun and charming. Your associations with loved ones can even improve incredibly. However, you need to venture out to pursue a class.

Showing your ways that will permit you to turn out to be less irate throughout everyday life and numerous circumstances that surface. Since we as a whole realize that outrage isn't useful for an individual. Numerous individuals who have outrage issues can have cardiovascular failure or even experience the ill effects of nervousness.

Relatively few individuals will consider that reality when they think about their outrage issues. In any case, as an observer to what that outrage can do face to face, it's an alarming actuality to feel that numerous individuals don't think they have an issue. In any event, overlook their family's requests now and again because they would prefer not to concede they have an issue.

Numerous methods will be utilized to assist you in figuring out how to unwind and control your displeasure. Something or other is a basic breathing strategy that you can utilize, and the tallying to ten stunts.

Another extraordinary strategy is figuring out how to unwind, be it music or something different that will permit you to remove your brain from the issue. Humor or chuckling is an incredible method to very quickly begin feeling the indignation sneak away.

Figuring out how to get decisive instead of blowing up will assist numerous individuals. You can prepare yourself to react thusly as opposed to getting offended. Now and again, one will bounce to outrage since they misconstrue a circumstance, all things considered, practice better correspondence.

On different occasions, it may be the case that the individual over responds to an issue. Practice improving correspondence with everyone around you to evade this event. As you discover what makes you vexed, you can likewise dodge those things.

3 tips to reduce anger

Outrage is one of the most tormenting infirmities to your psyche habitually whenever when the individual leaves states of mind. It is related to a profoundly unreasonable misdirected mind, making trouble mental self-view, and harming others. Irate upheavals influence contrarily one's associations with family and neighbors around known or obscure. An individual with outrage merits to no end well of his occupations. One is protected with base information on outrage by the board methods to lessen outrage.

Impacts of outrage

Much like stress and nervousness, outrage has a significant negative impact on the body against looking after wellbeing. Organic portrayal calls attention to that the mind is invigorated to instigate pituitary organs for the unnecessary discharge of hormones promptly to influence pretty much all aspects of the body. The impact of hormonal over-discharge keeps on flooding around the body and creates an expanded heartbeat, suffocation in the lungs, expanded typical glucose levels, and hypertension with the raised internal heat level.

Religion and outrage pressure the board

Practically all religions accentuate that outrage is the primary adversary with the individual involving a concealed spot and blasting out in outlandish circumstances. There is no issue until it is covered up and dozing at an oblivious level. When it develops with no explanation or for reasons unknown, the individual is obligated to endure the terrible impacts. From strict bearing, mental and handy physical bothers should be considered, and fundamental prudent indignation lessening steps should be taken.

Outrage decreasing tips

1. The prime indignation of the executives' instrument is to withdraw and reconsider before responding to state anything so you are sheltered from lamenting later.

2. Try not to resentment with others yet attempt to excuse since it is exceptionally nonsensical to anticipate that everybody should carry on decidedly in your line.

3. Humor is the best outrage decreasing procedure by envisioning yourself in clownish play with outrage.

4. Attempting to react rather than respond immediately to outrage triggers and stressors.

5. Leave yourself from the bewildering scene until you decide to react liberated from outrage. You can more readily have a connection with somebody you trust for exhortation.

To place practically speaking displeasure, the executive's procedures might be troublesome at musings and may require time and endeavors when confronting circumstances, sending you in rage. You may not be at your peak for adapting to the methodologies and following the tips to diminish outrage. The inner self-supporting annoyance ought to be lost and contemplate the serene life you're to appreciate thusly.

CHAPTER 29:

Verbal and nonverbal communication

Verbal and nonverbal communication has been seen to increase the ability of our social relationships. When verbal and nonverbal communication are not combined correctly, miscommunication can occur, leading to mental, physical, and emotional strain on the individual. Verbal communication is used when you are trying to convey a message through speech, writing, or sign language. Nonverbal communication is the messages you send out through your actions, such as facial expressions or gestures.

An example of verbal communication could be saying hello to a person you pass in the hallway at work with no response from them, which leads to a feeling of awkwardness between yourself and that person even though nothing was said (Haywood). An example of nonverbal communication could be someone you are trying to get to know at work walking into a meeting late, which makes you feel inconsiderate or not paying attention to what is being said. Anxieties can be formed in relationships when miscommunication involves verbal and nonverbal communication. Verbal and nonverbal communication directly affect our cognitive processes (Hodgins).

The first factor that verbal and nonverbal communication affects is the way we perceive things around us. This process contains two main parts, the cognitive interpretation of the stimulus and the affective response (Hodgins). The cognitive interpretation of the stimulus is when a person is trying to determine how they feel about what is being said or how they are being treated, and then they come up with emotion. The affective response deals with how the stimulus makes you feel. When you go into a conversation, you already have a plan for what you will say and how you are going to say it. If someone is giving off nonverbal signals that tell otherwise, such as shaking their head or crossing their arms, these actions will trigger your feelings differently than if there were no signals sent off (Hodgins).

The second factor that verbal and nonverbal communication can affect is our perception of ourselves. Our perception of ourselves can come from previous experiences, stereotypes that we hold, and how we feel about other people. One experience someone might have had is when they were a child. If they were never treated properly by their parents and were constantly called names at home or school, they might look at themself as being worthless. A stereotype that someone might believe is when you meet someone and think of them as fat because that has been your stereotype for years based on what you have seen on television (Hodgins). The way someone feels when they interact with another person is also something verbal and nonverbal communication effects (Hodgins). If someone does not like a certain person, they might treat them differently than how they would want to be treated by that person.

Lastly, verbal and nonverbal communication affects our learning and developing relationships. These two aspects of life can intertwine since you can learn more about people when you are putting yourself in their shoes (Hodgins). In the first example of verbal communication, you could not tell someone how you feel about them because you do not know how they will respond to what is being said. In the second example of verbal communication, if there were nonverbal communication between people, an uncomfortable environment would arise where nothing was being accomplished at the meeting. Both examples show how verbal and nonverbal communication change how you interact with others and how you feel about yourself.

Communication plays a key role in any relationship; it can keep us feeling like we are part of a social group or make us feel alienated from our peers. When we communicate, most people have nonverbal cues that they send out to let the other person know what is going on in their mind. Some things like facial expressions or gestures are hard to hide when they show what you think about someone or something that is being said (Hodgins). Besides the physical cues that are sent out, there are also verbal cues that can affect how another person feels during an interaction (Meyer). Verbal communication will send signals to someone that you are either trying to get to know them better or saying something that is not true. If the verbal cues are not being sent out correctly, then misinterpretation between two people can happen. People who have anxiety disorders are more sensitive to what others say and do. This can lead to them feeling uncomfortable around others (Barlow).

CHAPTER 30:

Apologize when is correct to do so

Many people are searching for "when to apologize," but it is often necessary to analyze and understand the context of the situation before you can take this decision.

Finally, if you do decide to apologize, keep in mind that this is not about whether you are "sorry" for your misbehavior or behavior. Many parents feel guilty for being rude or forgetful with their children and then try to apologize to reduce their guilty feelings.

Also, if you had misunderstood how someone has felt or acted (for example, thinking that they were criticized when they were only complaining about something), saying sorry will not affect the person's true feelings towards you. Independently of what you have done wrong, apologizing will not change their opinion of you if that person does not like (or trust) you.

In the following essay, I want to argue that the most important thing when dealing with people is to be consistent in your behavior and avoid hypocrisy. One of the best ways to achieve this is to eliminate all rules about what should be done and not be done in each situation. Instead, concentrate on being conscious about how your actions affect others and then try to be fair in your relationships. Suppose someone is trying to ruin your relationship because they feel jealous. In that case, it's because they feel insecure about their powers or qualities and don't feel secure enough about themselves.

When we are trying to apologize, we are trying to confuse our relationships, and we are projecting more blame. There is no conscious person who is not looking for a person who can criticize them. The only thing that matters is how often you will be criticized by people you love or feel close to you.

Everyone knows the term "I'm sorry" combined with a hug, but this is just an illusion of security when your biggest mistake was to feel guilty for your own mistakes. I'm not saying that you should go through life without making any mistakes or regrets, but it's better to deal with this differently. There is never a wrong time to apologize; if you think there is something you could have done differently, just let it go because the only time that matters is the present moment.

If your relationship is important to you, you should treat your relationship as important for your partner and not focus on how things should be or should not be. To achieve this, I recommend that you focus on making decisions that will make both of you happier and less stressed out about things like apologizing. In my opinion, it's better to make mistakes than to let the mistakes control your life.

Apologizing is only required when you are conscious of your actions. It's impossible to apologize for something you have not done, so don't worry if your partner doesn't forgive you. The goal of apologizing is to move on and feel better when someone criticizes you for something you have done wrong. If your partner loves you, they will find a better way to deal with things in the future.

Finally, I recommend that you make any decision only after careful consideration of its impact on other people around you and then act in a way that will be desired by others and yourself while trying not to judge others if they make different decisions than yours. If you commit to a decision that allows you to do so, there is no reason to apologize or regret it later.

CHAPTER 31:

Always be honest

The formation of a strong, healthy, and intimate relationship requires one to share secrets and experiences with their partner. In a good relationship, one should talk about things they cannot share with someone else. The kind of intimate, intense, and sensitive interchange in a healthy relationship requires the two parties to be honest with one another. Honesty involves sharing accurate information about an event or situation.

Honesty involves telling the truth as a whole. It has to be factual, and nothing is held back. In a healthy relationship, partners do not give misleading information knowingly. However, being honest does not entail insulting others, being unkind, rude, or aggressive. It does not involve spilling your guts just to hurt your partner. Honesty involves discretion; it is the ability to use good judgment over revealing or concealing. Discretion is very essential for a healthy relationship.

So, as much as you want to be honest, it is wrong to make rude remarks about your partner's new dressing code or the social class of another man/woman. It is not necessary to share feelings that might hurt your partner. You do not have to tell your partner that they are not hot enough, which is why you are leaving them. You can simply say that you need a break.

Besides, being honest does not mean sharing every other detail with your partner. It is okay to have some information you prefer not to share. Someone might have requested you to keep certain information a secret, and you have to respect that. Hold back the things you are not comfortable sharing. One day, you will be comfortable enough to speak about them.

A relationship is not a jail. Therefore, you have the right to withhold information if a question is asking for too much. You can choose to be vague or answer partially until you are ready to give all the information. However, do not lie. If a person is forcing you to reveal information, which you were asked not to share, you can say something like "That information is private, the person asked me to keep it secret, and therefore, it cannot be disclosed."

It is also okay to talk about your ambitions, goals, intentions, and targets in good faith. And you do not have to achieve everything you talk about. That is not lying. If you realize you might not keep your word for any reason, it is important to inform your partner. Try to find a viable solution that protects you and your partner, has the best interest, and respects the relationship.

People trust their loved ones unless they find out a lie. If someone violates the code of honesty, there is no sure way of knowing if they will repeat it. As such, people have a hard time trusting a person who lies. That is why cheating destroys so much, and it is impossible to repair. Any partners who want to remain in a relationship strongly must remain honest with one another and maintain goodwill and trust.

Honesty will make or break your relationship, and when your partner knows that they can truly trust you, it strengthens your bond. Knowing that you trust your mate completely b removes a large segment of worry in a relationship. Honesty does not only build your internal security but also makes you feel better about life. A good, healthy, and happy relationship creates a kind of buffer\wall between you and worldly worries. Having an honest and trustworthy mate also helps us to take on the risks of life with confidence.

A large number of people feel that occasional small lies that help to protect a partner are allowed. In some cases, that is true; you can spare a person pain by lying about some things. However, it is advisable to avoid lying. If you must, leave out the whole information or only share what is true. It is very hard to keep a culture of honesty, sometimes while lying on other occasions. If you opt to color, the truth by hiding the things that might hurt your partner, then you might damage your relationship at the core.

The need to protect your partner can cause more harm than good and create more trouble than it deserves. It is best to be smart in all your dealings.

Most of us will put honesty at the top of the list of things we want in our partners. Unfortunately, many of us have been lied to. Therefore, we know the pain and trauma. In a relationship, the two people need to know that they are on the same page, thus the need for honesty.

Honesty gives a person the comfort of knowing that they can trust their partner. The knowledge that two people are truly open with each other will make a relationship last. So, if you want a lasting relationship, maintain honesty and trust. You will be able to share positive energy when in a positive relationship.

Share your truth in a way that benefits your partner. We like to hear about our strengths and positive side, but it is helpful to mention what we need to change. If you are advising or correcting your partner, do it gently. And there is nothing stronger than the advice of someone we love and trust. Honesty needs to be helpful and tender. If you must say something that might undo your partner, be kind. Use some degree of maturity in your words.

Brutal honesty is advocated for a lot these days. However, it has caused more harm than good in most cases. Brutal honesty tends to cause wounds in our hearts, thus making it hard to have constructive conversations. Avoid it.

Note that honesty is not just a behavior; it is a lifestyle, a way to happiness. Keep it paramount in your relationship, and you will keep the bad stuff out. Honesty and trust bring in positive things. Knowing that there is trust between you and your spouse will offer you comfort and freedom that helps to build your relationship.

CHAPTER 32:

Have fun together

A lot of us find it challenging to have fun with our partners. Sometimes, we are too shy to express ourselves freely.

It varies from one person to another on how they express themselves. Some people are talkative and open-minded when they are in a relationship, while others become withdrawn and quiet when in one.

The danger lies when you don't express your feelings and thoughts to your partner; for example, you feel hurt but don't tell your partner why you felt that way and instead bottle up inside, which may cause even more problems. It's one thing if you need some time to sort out your feelings and thoughts, but it is also when dealing with your partner. Sometimes it isn't even that bad; they just find it difficult while having fun with their partners because they are too focused on enjoying their time alone and do not want the other person to get in the way of what they're doing or saying.

It does vary from one person to another on how they express themselves when in a relationship. If you feel you are too distant from your partner, try to express yourself more openly and freely. If you find it hard to express yourself or be more open with your partner, you should look at the root of the problem.

Sometimes we bottle up everything inside us that we have no idea what's wrong with us. We just get used to being in denial about our feelings that, at one point, it becomes difficult for us to tell ourselves what is wrong with us and why we feel a certain way about something because we don't even know ourselves.

When in a relationship, you should be able to feel comfortable around your partner and express yourself freely and openly. If you feel you're too quiet in the relationship, talk to your partner and tell them what's wrong, so they won't think there is something wrong with them or the relationship.

Talking it out may help with your feelings for each other, but it isn't an instant fix-all solution; it takes time, like any other relationship. You need to make time for each other to improve your communication skills. It does take time to learn how to express yourself freely without holding back or being afraid of saying something wrong. Expressing yourself freely can be difficult when you're not used to doing it often. But it isn't always about how you express yourself with your partner; you have to do the same with your friends too because many people find it difficult to express themselves freely or open up to their friends and family. You don't necessarily need to talk every time you meet up with them; some of us prefer texting our friends or hanging out alone while texting our friends at the same time. Expressing yourself is an essential part of any relationship, whether it is romantic, partnership, friendship, or otherwise. You should express yourself freely to let your partner know how you feel about something and whether you are comfortable with what they are doing.

If you can't do it, work on it slowly. Don't put too much pressure on yourself because, at the end of the day, it's about enjoying your relationship (whether romantic or otherwise) and not about being perfect.

When in a relationship, learn to be open, honest, and caring toward each other. Learn to show affection to one another by holding hands or just sitting together in silence, content that you're together and happy together.

CHAPTER 33:

Find common interests

A the common reason for anxiety in relationships is the lack of common interests. When you get together with your friends, you usually do the same things—you love to go shopping, swimming, and play sports. You have the same hobbies and things you enjoy doing with them, such as going to parties and taking part in dinner. You also have similar goals in life: getting a good job, getting married, and starting a family. And this is what binds you together.

These shared interests help to reduce anxiety in relationships. You understand yourself and others around you better because you know what they are interested in and compare them with you. When you and your friend have something in common, it is easier for you to understand each other and feel that this person is similar to you, "Yes, we are all the same, we're just like him." Feeling that a person is identical to us helps to reduce anxiety. The more interests we have in common, the more relaxed we are. Also, if a person shares our interests, then this person is less likely to offend or criticize us. We may think, "He has similar dreams as me; he will not hurt me."

Thus, common interests provide a reasonable basis for relationships. We all want our friends. We want to know their interests to feel closer to them, but often we do not know how to find this out. This is why we will tell you how to do it! The first question you should ask yourself as soon as possible is, "What are my interests?" Write down everything that comes to your mind in a notebook.

You will need it in the future. Then write down the main interests of your friends, because they will be useful to you. Then ask your friends what their interests are. It's not difficult if you know how to do this! Start with small talk about topics that are interesting for the first, for example, "I'm going on vacation soon, I'm very excited."

"What kind of books do you like?" "What places have you been to?" "What is your most favorite sport?" When you find out their interests, tell them about your hobbies and interests!

What can I do to find out about my friend's interests? If you want to know what your friends are interested in, think about what you have in common with them. You have something in common with everyone!

Find out what you already have in common by talking with your friends: "What music would you listen to during your free time?" "Which movies would you like to watch?" Find out what kind of books they read. Start reading more, go to the library, and borrow books. If you see that your friends read interesting books—start reading them yourself! Who knows, maybe this book is interesting for them? Ask them if they agree. If you like to read the same thing, you can start a reading group to discuss the books. You can also share your hobbies and go to places where you both enjoy spending time. When we have a lot in common with friends, we are more relaxed and willing to communicate, which helps us get along better with each other.

It's essential that you don't look at your friend only from the point of view of whether they will be the right dating partner for you—because if they do not show any interest in you, it does not mean that it's impossible to find friendship and establish an emotional connection with them.

CHAPTER 34:

Make projects and set goals together

To succeed in a relationship, you should realize what you need in any part of life. While you may discover a good relationship out of blind luckiness, being clear about your objective helps a lot. You can use this skill to get you on the right path and to control your end route.

In broad terms, what makes for a safe relationship in youth likewise makes for a secure relationship in adulthood.

So, you can consider relationships having these three associated essential qualities:

- **Emotional accessibility:** children need their folks genuinely and sincerely near to assist them in having a sense of safety, yet grown-up relationships are more reliant on the partners' sincere close. While partitions and significant distance can cause stress in romantic relationships, they are not significant. However, partners must acknowledge and be receptive to one another's needs. When your partner stays far off, you will probably feel alone, dismissed, or relinquished, and may scrutinize your incentive as an individual.

- **Place of refuge:** just as a kid runs back to his/her mom when undermined or vexed, partners in a healthy relationship go to one another when they need consolation or backing during troublesome occasions. Since life is turbulent, it's essential to have a partner who can offer support, help, and relief from those challenges. Individuals who realize they have this trusted "port in a tempest" are less overwhelmed by life's difficulties.

- **A secure base:** to feel satisfied throughout everyday life and adored in a relationship, it's significant for individuals to have the option to seek after their deep desires—or even just to have the opportunity to investigate what those needs might be. Healthy relationships are ones in which partners empower and bolster those endeavors.

As you consider these characteristics of a healthy relationship, remember that the two partners need to cooperate to make them possible. Partners should be able to tolerate and be tolerated, which is fundamental to emotional accessibility; to comfort and be comforted, guaranteeing a place of refuge in a difficult situation; and to empower and be empowered, making the relationship a safe base from which to investigate the world. Even though you are presumably more worried about having a partner offering these "blessings" to you, it is similarly significant for him/her to have the option to get them because it's an open give-and-take dynamic that sustains relationships. So, also, it is fundamental that you are fit for offering and accepting these things.

What to look for in a partner

The right partner can achieve to be the individual you want to be. Specialists Drigotas, Rusbult, Wieselquist, and Whitton distinguished and discovered help for this procedure, named the Michelangelo marvel. Much like Michelangelo would, through chiseling, draw out the beautiful forms that he could find in a block of stone before him, a caring partner can draw out your ideal or "perfect" self and uncover this lovely nature in you.

The partner you need

- **Safely attached and mature.** Since such individuals are ok with themselves and their relations, they are fit for being sincerely close. They are likewise ready to consider themselves and their lives in an open, creative, and openly associated way. This empowers them to recognize their impediments and non-defensively admit to their mix-ups—all without yielding a positive feeling of themselves. Understanding that others are also defective, they can promptly pardon their partners.

- **A viable communicator.** Such partners are acceptable at tuning in and sharing, encouraging them to support and keep up cozy relationships. They can likewise successfully work through contradictions. To some extent, they have these qualities since they commonly distinguish and man maturing their feelings.

- **Keen to you.** It isn't sufficient to experience emotional feelings for someone. You need a partner that respects and empowers you—and attempts to communicate this in a way or another. Your partner must show enthusiasm for becoming more acquainted with you. You will then be more joyful and arrive at your most prominent potential with help and support to investigate your advantages.

- **A healthy match.** It is imperative to participate in getting to know each other. It all starts with some mutual interests, and it certainly implies involvement from both parties in understanding each other, regardless of whether that just includes having drawn-in discussions. Sharing each other's qualities is significant for a drawn-out relationship. Furthermore, the more those qualities influence everyday life, the more significant it is to share. For example, fiasco anticipates when one partner is resolved to have kids, and the other partner is totally against it. Then, if one partner is focused on a migrant way of life, the relationship boat will work much better if the other partner is strong.

- **You are prepared for a relationship.** Your partner must be eager to focus on the relationship. This implies committing time and concentrating on it when you are together and separated. It likewise includes seeing sex and emotional closeness as two parts of a personal relationship that help one another. Finally, a possible right partner will accept that you—as a team—are liable for one another's bliss.

- **Recollect that you don't have to discover mr. Or ms. Great (neither of those individuals exists or mr. Or ms. Ideal for-me.)** That can end up being an endless hunt with the steady expectation of finding a superior individual practically around the bend. What you have to discover is mr./ms. Bravo. I am not saying that you have to settle for somebody you are not so much content with, but instead that you ensure you have your needs straight.

One last thing

Don't rush to move past a "pleasant, however exhausting" date. As Levine and Heller (2010) note, individuals often compare their relationship-related tension with the feeling of being infatuated. When somebody is agreeable to being with you and appears to tolerate you, your relationship-related nervousness probably won't be activated. So, it's conceivable that the "good individual" you met maybe an incredible fit for you—notwithstanding the absence of quick "fervor."

CHAPTER 35:

Fight the monotony in intimacy

Learn from history

Instead of letting history define you, you can take the opportunity to learn something from it to conquer your fear of intimacy. Take a few moments to think about your past relationships and answer the following questions:

- What were the stumbling blocks?

- Where did it go wrong?

- What are the significant issues that continuously come up in all your relationships?

- What thoughts led to these problems in your relationships?

- What did you tell yourself whenever your significant other expressed their emotions, talked about severe plans in a relationship, asked how you felt about them?

- What did you tell yourself whenever your partner rescheduled date night for the next day, said something wrong, or didn't stay overnight when you asked them to?

Once you determine the patterns that show up in every relationship, it will be easier for you to trace them back to their roots and discover the underlying cause of your fear of intimacy.

Tell your inner critic to "shut up"

Remember that voice in your head continually nags and tells you your partner doesn't like you, they don't find you attractive; you don't deserve happiness, etc.? Well, this inner critic coaches you to avoid feeling intimate or vulnerable, which affects your relationships. The inner critic tries to lure you away from finding love, destroys your confidence and self-esteem, and makes you feel bad about yourself and your partners. In turn, you refuse to give a chance to love and have the urge to escape whenever you feel like a specific relationship will become more emotional and intimate.

Refusing to listen to your inner critic is an essential step towards conquering your fears. You can do so in many ways. For example, you can come up with your mantra to tell yourself why you deserve love, why someone likes you, etc. Furthermore, for every evil thought that your inner critic creates in your mind, find an answer that negates it. For example, whenever you think, "he doesn't like you," you should immediately respond, "he's with me; he likes me. There are many reasons one could like me..." The point here is to eliminate self-destructive thoughts and reduce their intensity to accept love and everything that comes with it.

Feel your feelings

Love-making feel alive isn't just a cliché that you see in romantic comedies; it's entirely true. Love makes us feel different things and emotions. However, it makes us prone to potential pain and loss at the same time. Does the possibility of being rejected or broken up have to stop you from feeling all your feelings when you are in a relationship? No, of course not.

If you don't accept the possibility that you might experience pain and loss, you will also reject all good things that come with love, strong and healthy relationships. Plus, pain and loss might not even happen. Since we don't know what the future holds, we should embrace love, happiness, joy, passion, laughter, and all things love offers instead of hiding.

Therefore, to conquer your fear of intimacy, letting yourself feel your feelings is a must. A strong and healthy relationship is a result of the freedom to experience different feelings and emotions.

This can also teach you how to embrace different opportunities in life as well. Being scared of failure doesn't let you advance in your career, which also implies your romantic life. Newfound freedom will motivate you to explore and allow yourself to feel things that you have never felt before. Love is the only thing that can do that.

Be vulnerable

Most people constantly live in fear of being vulnerable. Why not? who likes to be weak? That's what you're probably thinking right now. But being vulnerable isn't the same as being weak. Being vulnerable is a mark of strength, not weakness. Being vulnerable means that you decide to ignore those voices in your head, the inner critics, and act the way you feel. Only when you are vulnerable and open can you survive and have a strong relationship with your partner. Benefits of being vulnerable include:

Being vulnerable means you decide to ignore those voices in your head, the inner critics, and act the way you feel.

- Life is filled with honesty towards yourself and other people.

- A broad spectrum of possibilities.

- Opportunity to love and be loved.

- Knowing that you are always yourself, regardless of the situation, good or bad.

- Breaking old patterns that held you back before.

When you allow yourself to be vulnerable and more open, you finally admit that you are the one who controls your happiness. Only when you accept that will you be able to embrace what your partner brings into your relationship.

Writing down your fears

This might sound to you like a weird way of dealing with the fear of intimacy, but it's quite effective. After all, the most effective way of reaching some specific goal is by writing it down and keeping it as a reminder. This isn't much different either. Here is how to do it:

- Take a blank piece of paper.

- Write down signs and symptoms of intimacy anxiety, even those that you consider unimportant.

- Write down why you feel what you feel—this will lead you to underlying causes.

- Write down the reasons you discover.

- Add goals you want to accomplish.

Keep the list as a reminder that you will take action against your fear of intimacy and work towards resolving it. This list can also serve as a motivation. Acknowledging fear of intimacy, defining symptoms and causes is already a giant leap towards a more vigorous exercise.

You can also opt to write a letter to yourself and your partner. In the letter, you should write about your intimacy anxiety, how it makes you feel, and why. You should also include reasons you want to build a strong relationship and a few ideas to help you accomplish that. Writing things down is a therapeutic way of de-stressing and acknowledging emotions that you didn't even know existed.

Define what you want

Trying to change something about yourself is not the easiest thing in the world. You can't banish fear of intimacy overnight, but you can handle the entire process a lot easier by defining what you want. This can also be included in writing yourself a letter or list about your intimacy anxiety. Take a few moments to think about what you want from a relationship. Of course, we are on the road to building a strong and healthy relationship, but every person has their definition of a strong relationship. You should add this info to the list. Plus, if your partner already offers what you want from your relationship, this will make you appreciate them more. On the other hand, if you're single and want to know how to build a strong relationship, this particular detail can help you identify what you're looking for.

Socialize, connect

To conquer your fears of intimacy, you have to socialize and connect with other people. First, you can't spend your entire life in your home. Second, you can't beat intimacy anxiety if you aren't comfortable around a larger group of people. When you do that, you will see how easy it is to be yourself and express your feelings, emotions, and desires to one particular person only. Plus, going out and socializing is an excellent way of meeting new potential partners if you are still single.

Don't worry, be happy

Remember, life is too short to be serious, sad, and push people away all the time. Learn to let go and have fun. Sometimes, your fear of intimacy doesn't allow you to relax and be yourself. Discover a whole new world when you loosen up and decide to enjoy life, love, and everything they bring.

Be curious

Intimacy doesn't only refer to physical relations with your significant other. It also means connecting with that person on a deeper, emotional level. The only way to truly feel close to someone is by being curious and getting to know them better. You can find out more about a person by having one of those conversations where you tell each other everything, taking a trip, signing up for some class together, etc. Sharing various experiences will help you connect with someone emotionally and be more relaxed, which is the ultimate way of conquering the fear of intimacy.

CHAPTER 36:

Anxiety in intimacy

What is intimacy?

D o you ask, "What does intimacy mean?" Intimacy is an act of love that goes way beyond physics. It's a feeling of well-being in a relationship, mentally and emotionally. It's a profound bond we have with someone else that helps us to appreciate our relationship and affection for them well.

Intimacy requires a degree of mutual security. It attempts on a foundational basis to fulfill the wishes of both parties. It needs couples to be transparent and honest with each other, depending on the absolute love that a couple has.

Intimacy is not just a one-act play. It is a constant, conscious endeavor. Whether the day is positive or bad, it expresses in relationships ups and downs. The passion is specifically intended for those who wish to try love and work hard to make it the center of their relationship.

What is not intimacy

You aren't fond of other things. They often associate love with the shallow elements of marriages, and so they often see it represented.

Hold this in mind when determining if you have intimacy in your relationship:

- **Intimacy is not just sex.** While the physical aspects of a relationship can improve intimacy, intimacy usually does not survive in a relationship lacking a deeper connection. Because these two go hand in hand, their meaning can be quickly mistaken. Note, sex may fulfill a physical need, but love often serves physical, social, and intellectual needs.

- **Intimacy is not a gift.** Although meeting our partner's desires is a vital component of a healthy relationship, and doing something that those we love can do, confidence is not buying or selling. Gift-giving, lavish trips, and expensive dates are not a good base for romance.

- **Intimacy is not a fairytale.** Both relationships have their ups and downs, and there will be love, given the ups and downs, in truly intimate relations. It is fun to be swept up in a dramatic storm and fall in love. Yet if those butterfly feelings start to fade slowly and the relationship continues to die with them, chances are that passion has not played as much of a role as it should have.

Do you have an intimate relationship?

Intimacy is different in any arrangement because no two parties are the same. Yet being able to answer "yeah" to the following questions is a good indication that your relationship is on the right track:

- Does decision-making matter for both you and your partner?

- Would you spend time discussing shared desires with your partner?

- Do you and your partner make communications a priority?

- Do you accept each other as you are?

- Do you seek a physical connection with your partner?

- Should you and your friend chat together about hopes, ambitions, and fears?

- Do you support one another and your partner in their goals?

- Do you treat each other with love?

- Do you and your partner consistently express love for each other?

- Do you encourage each other to keep yourselves individual?

- Do you have inside jokes with your partner?

- Are you the "go-to" with your partner when things get tough?

- Would you make room for each other and your family without distractions?

- Do you understand each other's "non-verbal" communication?

- Do you and your friend take advantage of the chance to converse or share time during the day?

Answering "yes" to each of those questions is a sure indication that the intimacy of friendship flourishes. It is accomplished by couples whose marriages have a high degree of trust due to having open lines of contact, empathy, and mutual agreement.

Despite what happens in the relationship, both partners value one another and continuously inspire each other to do what matters to them. Extremely intimate relationships consider the spouse's interests and encourage parties to lobby in the connection for their rights.

Real romantic relationships create a safe atmosphere for both sides and deliberately try to maintain that sense of protection. Remember that physically, mentally, and emotionally, this occurs periodically.

Keep in mind

When you find yourself answering these questions with more "no's" than you would like, then it is time to look at your needs again. But don't worry; answering "no" to any of the questions mentioned above doesn't mean it would spoil your relationship. There's not a relationship going on. The questions you answered "no" to will act as a starting point for a conversation with your partner and will bring you to a consensus about what your potential relationship looks like. Keep in mind that any connection to the idea of "intimate" is remarkable. When you and your wife do not answer "yes" to these questions but are otherwise happy with your relationship, this may mean that all of your contact needs are not being fulfilled. Don't forget: one person in a relationship may feel as if their needs are being met, while their partner doesn't feel the same. You must contact your partner here. You have to fight for yourself and your rights because you think your friend has a layer you don't fulfill.

How can you make the relationship more intimate?

Just because you believe there is a lack of trust in your friendship doesn't mean you and your partner are ruined. Creating love in a relationship is a cycle, and it takes time to build the foundation for individual partnerships. You can do other things to make the friendship more personal, including:

1. **Use relationships to teach you how to be whole within:** relationships are not about making anyone full of you, but about belonging to the whole community and interdependent sharing of your life. By letting go of the unrealistic dream of meeting and being "one," as rainer maria rilke terms it, you understand the differences between intimacy and solidarity.

2. **See your partner for exactly who they are:** the sentimental tragedy is that you see the person you love as a reflection of their dreams and what they have come to represent. You keep figuring out who they are and how they grow and improve as you remember that you don't even know your partner any better than you do.

3. **Be willing to learn from each other:** the trick is to look at the other as a mirror and learn how to be a healthier person from the suggestions. Instead of blaming your friend and scratching your fists, stay awake while you're upset over what's yet to be resolved inside.

4. **Get comfortable being alone:** get ready to spend time with yourself and know that love can't save you by itself. By feeling secure within the relationship structure, you will become more whole, relaxed, and ready to be on your own.

5. **Look closely at why a fight might begin:** some couples establish supremacy by battle and then split up repeatedly. This helps to maintain the impression of passion, creating anticipation and removing real intimacy. Once you realize what you're scared of in general, you'll have a better sense of why you're struggling—and you'll be battling for less.

CHAPTER 37:

Understand if your partner is only interested in sex and what to do

O ne way of minimizing the risk of intimacy is to move slowly, take "baby steps," and watch your partner respond. Think about tiny ways you could be a little more intimate. Maybe you will share a bit of what you thought. You might say, for example, "I'm a grumpy little today," "I 'm concerned about XYZ," "I feel really in love with you," or "I'm angry about ABC." Or maybe you might reveal a sincere viewpoint rather than biting your tongue or saying something you don't believe. Or you could tell any of your dreams or expectations or ambitions to your friend, rather than holding them to yourself.

Note your partner's reactions when you take such slight risks. Those are positive indicators if they react with honesty, compassion, engagement, and acceptance; they mean you can trust them. Those are not positive signs if they react with aggression, isolation, disdain, disinterest, or rejection; these reactions can only undermine confidence. The same holds when the other foot is on the shoe. When your wife starts opening up to you, keep her free. React entirely to mind: lookout with transparency and interest. Tune in your contributions, connections, and caring values. By giving your wife a "safe place" to open up, you're adding to her safety and well-being, creating a meaningful bond, and demonstrating that you care.

Why do you create a room like that? First, defuse assumptions, critiques, and other unhelpful things that pop into your mind automatically; just note those feelings and let them come and go. Second, indulge in: put your complete knowledge of what your partner says and does; make him the object of your concern. Thirdly, it shows you love. One especially effective way to do this is to create a healthier sex life through a method called "validation."

Building a better sex life

Many people divide their relationship arbitrarily into two parts:

1. The sex-life.

2. Everything else.

Even the separation is unhelpful. Generally speaking, it's more helpful to think about sex as just one thing that helps you interact pleasurably. Some people believe that they will be able to have a fantastic sex life given a miserable current relationship—full of disconnection, reactivity, and avoidance. Think about it once again! Although you may consider unusual examples, usually, if there is a significant DRAIN in your relationship—disconnection, reactivity, denial, inside your mind, neglecting values—it affects your sex life adversely. After all, if you can't lovingly communicate outside of the bedroom, why would the inside be any different?

If your sex life is not as pleasant as a general rule, focus on repairing the DRAIN in other aspects of your relationship. This paves the way for a better, more enjoyable sex life as you reestablish caring, connection, compassion, and confidence. By contrast, if you try to fix your sex life while your relationship is full of tension, your chances of success are not very good. If your friendship thrives, you will add LOVE to improve your sex life—letting go, giving up, trusting, and connecting.

Sex and letting go

What unhelpful standards, rules, and judgments should you let go of to improve your sex life? Here are a few specific ones: Your wife will desire (or at least commit to) the same sexual behavior as you do.

You or your wife will have sex more often/less often. You should have a better erection or orgasm, or your wife would. You or your wife will get an erection or more easily/more often/faster/slowly achieve an orgasm.

If you combine those standards, you will feel fear, anger, or disappointment repeatedly. Why? For what? Since orgasms, erections, personal tastes, and sex-drive all differ greatly—not only from person to person but also from week to week and from day-to-day. And if you hold your desires too closely, it isn't going to be long before you're battling reality.

Sex and valuing

What are the ideals that underlie sex? Is it about communication, care, sensuality, physical pleasure sharing, sexual desire, and love affirmation? Many people wreck their sex lives by transforming sex into an operation based on the goal: it is all about the orgasm. Although getting an orgasm is usually a pleasurable experience, sooner or later, such an approach can cause complications until it is "the be-all and end-all" of your sex life.

Why? For what? And there are all kinds of times when you or your partner won't get an orgasm or an erection, or you'll come too soon, slowly or not at all. Different causes in your relationship include tiredness, fatigue, anxiety, exhaustion, physical illness, medications, alcohol, aging effects, or continuing conflict. Sometimes it happens for no good reason—"just because." Here's a common story: "The main point of sex is to reach orgasm, and unless that happens, it's not good sex!" If you cling to this story closely, what do you suppose would happen? This creates an intense atmosphere where there is real pressure to achieve your goal and to perform.

This, in effect, also contributes to "performance anxiety": a sense of discomfort or strain or fear of disappointment when you're having sex. And the dilemma is that when you're nervous or depressed, the reproductive organs "turn off," making it nearly difficult to achieve climax, regulate the ejaculation, or maintain an erection. Thus, the more pressure you have to "perform," the more often you will have sexual issues. Look at the endless loop, anybody? And if this pattern continues, one or both partners will start avoiding sex before long because it gets too full of bad feelings!

If you based your sex life on ideals rather than on goals, you could quickly break this revolving loop. Instead of dwelling on erections and orgasms, you should use sex as a means for your partner to communicate and care about him. You are home with that mindset. Connection and care can occur in many different ways, irrespective of whether you are getting an erection or having an orgasm.

Via kissing, embracing, rubbing, oral sex, grooming, taking a bath together, or snuggling all your clothing on the sofa, you will enact such principles! You could go to bed and enjoy the bodies of each other without ever having to engage in intercourse. You might try to touch each other in different ways to see if it feels pleasurable. You should seek to explore any part of your body, not just your breasts or vagina. Without really attempting to produce an orgasm, you could have intercourse: doing it solely and expressing pleasure or establishing a sense of connection. Your subconscious will think, of course, that's not real sex!—but what does it cost you to keep the one tight?

In all of this, one crucial thing to remember: the importance of love is utterly vital. Sex isn't going the way you'd expect. This is a given.

And if you get stuck within your head or turn into reactivity mode, when the unpleasant happens, then you can do or do all kinds of hurtful things that destroy trust and intimacy. That, in effect, will exacerbate your long-term sex life. The message is simple: settle your beliefs around caring and making sex free, whatever happens!

Sex and engaging

Caution can significantly improve physical contact. If you kiss, hug, caress, nuzzle, hold hands, rub, undress, embrace, or have foreplay, oral sex, or intercourse, mindfulness will intensify both the pleasure and the sense of deep attachment. As you tap into your own body's feelings and respond to your partner's responses, intercourse is an exciting experience—far more pleasurable than when you're just wrapped up in your mind or concentrated on reaching the orgasm target.

CHAPTER 38:

Ask yourself what your partner would do without your quality

W hile is natural to want to feel your partner's need, it's also important to realistically assess whether you are meeting a real need or if your contribution is more of a one-sided attachment. This is not necessarily a bad thing, particularly if you both feel secure and love being together. Many couples prefer each other's company to spend time with any other person. Generally, this is the kind of quality that will increase over time as long as both partners recognize the benefits of being together and appreciate what they have together. In a dysfunctional relationship, however, the feeling of being attached often holds one partner back from growing into a more independent person. There are many examples of an "attached" quality in a relationship, but one of the most common is when the dependent looks to the other for assurance that they are loved and valued. This may be demonstrated in a variety of ways. You can compare how often you value yourself when around your mate versus other people. Do you feel better about yourself because of your partner's admiration?

You might also consider how you experience anxiety or insecurity in your relationship. One of the primary ways in which you will experience anxiety is about intimacy. Your partner may be aware of this, and they may even try to "fix" it for you. But asking for reassurance from your partner helps make your anxiety worse and decreases your ability to be more confident, independent, and intimate. It is very unhealthy to rely on a partner for feeling good about yourself. Other examples of an attached quality include finding love through making sacrifices or being needed by your partner and using this as a basis for feeling valuable. All these qualities are forms of codependent relationships that focus on giving up something of yourself to feel loved. As you can see, it's easy to define what an attached quality looks like, but harder to determine its presence in your life. An attached quality is a form of addiction, so it is often difficult to notice because you think that it is normal to feel secure in the relationship and need your partner. It may feel nice when your partner is attentive and shows signs of caring. However, if you look at attachment from a negative perspective, you can see how unhealthy it is.

Discovering the meaning behind your need to be attached

The first step in discovering whether your relationship includes an attached quality is identifying why you might feel insecure without it. Are you truly dependent on your partner? Are there situations that make you feel this way? Perhaps your partner has a history of not being there for you or not showing up when you needed them. Or maybe other people in your life have demonstrated an unreliable quality, such as parents, friends, employers, or coworkers. If so, this could cause you to be overly dependent on the closest person to you. Another clue that your relationship includes an attached quality is thinking about how you feel about yourself when you are with your partner versus other people. Do you feel more confident and secure when you are with your mate? Or does your self-esteem increase because of the way they value and praise you? If so, this feeling comes from a good place but still demonstrates a poorer quality than feeling good about yourself independent of a relationship. If you find yourself answering these questions in the affirmative and are concerned about having an attached quality, you can take steps to improve the situation. The first step is to understand why it exists in the first place: usually because something from the past has led to insecurity.

CHAPTER 39:

How to find bravery to exit from a relationship where you are chained

R elationship anxiety, in many ways, is distressing and burdensome. People suffer immensely when they are trapped in a relationship with an abusive partner or are deeply infected by the feeling of rejection or insecurity. While there is no 'quick-fix' solution to break this cycle of anxiety and stress associated with relationships, the first step towards a better future is to take charge of your life and take brave steps towards exiting from your present situation. The following set of strategies will help you find the courage to end relationships that leave you vulnerable or unhappy. It is important to remember that 'a relationship' only exists when you choose the other person as a lifetime partner. The moment you decide to end a relationship or break up because of an abusive situation, there is no more 'relationship' but just two individuals involved. While ending relationships that are beyond repair can be frightening and intimidating, support from family and friends, along with self-awareness, can help you find the right step towards healing and better relationships in the future.

Ending your present relationship

The first step towards exiting from an unhealthy relationship understands what 'healthy' means in a relationship context. Healthy relationships involve a significant degree of love, care, and respect for each other. A healthy relationship is not meant to control, manipulate, or influence the other person. Healthy love is about respecting and accepting each other as individuals. Healthy relationships are built on mutual trust and respect, and these relationships are managed through discussions and negotiations rather than fear, manipulation, and domination. One step towards ending a toxic relationship is to identify the unhealthy aspects of your present situation. List down all the qualities of your current relationship that make it sick (e.g., arguing too much, jealousy issues, lack of trust, etc.). Analyze the problem areas and reasons why your relationship is unhealthy. Depending on the situation, it could help discuss your concerns with a family member or a non-judgmental friend. You can also visit a counselor in this regard. While it is not easy to accept criticism of your present situation, it is essential to consider whether any of these 'issues' in themselves will be reason enough for you to decide to end your current relationship. Sometimes, people get into relationships because they feel lonely and crave companionship and affection. This aspect needs careful analysis as well before making any decision about ending the relationship.

Know your goals and reasons for leaving

You must know what you want from a relationship. Think about your aims and objectives from your present relationship. Evaluate your current relationship in light of the objectives mentioned above. What do you expect from your partner? Are you getting what you want? If not, why? Is it possible for your partner to give or improve on what you expect from them?

Find out whether you have done everything you could (e.g., tried to initiate a change of behavior, discussed issues with your partner, etc.) before deciding to end the relationship. It is important to remember that while relationships cannot be forced upon us, they can only grow and develop if people in a relationship actively and make their love work.

Conclusion

A problem-related to anxiety is the anxiety in relationships. This kind of anxiety takes the form of both a characteristic and a disorder.

In a characteristic, the person shows a significant amount of heightened anxiety when in relationships with others. This increased level of anxiety is present most or all the time but is not so high that it starts to cause problems in an individual's life. It just causes problems, specifically when interacting with others.

Two different types fall under this label: anxious attachment style and anxious-ambivalent attachment style, which are both characterized by excessive worry and concern about being rejected by other people in romantic relationships due to fear of being alone or losing important people in their lives.

Anxious attachment is characterized by a fear of rejection or abandonment by others in relationships and the high need for approval. People who have an anxious attachment style tend to be very dependent on their partner, worry about whether their partner still loves them, and are often jealous of their partner's relationships with other people. When faced with a crisis, they are generally anxious and pessimistic. Their partners most often feel detached from the relationship because they feel as though they are being smothered and held down by their excessive neediness.

Anxious-ambivalent attachment styles are characterized by feelings of jealousy and possessiveness in their relationships. They are often overly anxious about being rejected or abandoned by others and usually feel that they have to be extremely careful about what they say to them because they fear that other people will think badly of them because of it. They tend to become anxious when their partner goes out and tend to worry about why. People who have anxiously ambivalent attachment styles also tend to be overly sensitive about how their partner reacts toward them during social interactions with others or even when things are going well. These individuals tend to have a harder time communicating with their partners and effectively negotiating when the relationship is going through a rough patch. These are the two main subtypes of anxious attachment style.

According to the DSM-IV-TR (2000), individuals with a general anxious attachment style were found to be more likely, than those who did not have an anxious attachment style to engage in "pejorative" worry, which usually involves superstitious or unrealistic thoughts about events happening in one's life. These worries are usually unhelpful and are not a way of successfully preparing for future events. Anxious attachment individuals were also found to be less confident in the contexts of their relationships and more likely to be dissatisfied with their relationships than those who do not have an anxious attachment style.

Anxiety disorders include panic disorder, social anxiety disorder, specific phobias, obsessive-compulsive disorder, PTSD, and generalized anxiety disorders. It is common among children and adolescents, and 20% of women in the US suffer from Generalized Anxiety Disorder (GAD) at some point in their lives.